How To Make A Living By Working For Free

A HOW-TO GUIDE FOR ARTISTS TO CREATE A
COMMUNITY AROUND WHAT THEY DO ONLINE.

Simon Mark Caine

Copyright © 2016 Simon Mark Caine
All rights reserved.

ISBN: 1522925759
ISBN 13: 9781522925750

This book was funded via IndieGoGo in January 2016. Below are the names of the early backers who supported me and deserve recognition and thanks. Without these people who pre-ordered the book while it was in development I wouldn't have been able to complete this project, so sincerely, thank you.

Gemma Phelan.	Ross Hepburn.
Mike Sheldon.	Al Cowie.
Isabel Rees.	Donald Hamilton.
Hari Sriskantha.	Jason Simmons.
Sean Brightman.	Gareth Wilson.
Dave Parton.	Steve Titley.
Chris Lincé.	Steve Hili.
Jacob Hatton.	James Cocks.
Gav Cross.	Jasper.
Joshua Helmer.	Brendan Dowse.
Amir Sohi.	Sam Brady.
Chris Young.	Ben Jennings.
Ben Hall.	Chris Ryan.
Alasdair Beckett-King.	Alun Watkins.
James Cook.	Connor Kent.
Matt Hoss.	Sandy Wardrop.
Alfie Noakes.	Barry Davidson.
Richard Clarke.	Rachel Wheeley.
Pete Dunbar	James Hargreaves.

Introduction

This book is called How To Make A Living By Working For Free for two reasons -

1. it's about how you can make a living through free online content.
2. it's a catchy title.

Catchy titles are useful in publishing because they capture your imagination and help you (the reader) remember the name so if it comes up in conversation you can tell what book will help them - we'll cover how to stand out in someone's imagination later in the book.

Hi. My name is Simon. First of all, thanks for buying my book. It has taken me just over two years to put this together and frankly it was a long and painful process. So I'm just happy that you're able to read it as it has been sitting on my laptop's hard drive for way too long.

This book intends to tell you (yes you!) how you can make a living by working for free. It sounds mad, but bear with me.

In this book I intend to show you why finding an audience for your work has never been easier and the secrets behind making that happen (psst, the secret is it takes hard work and dedication... Where are you going? That's the secret but there's more to read about in this book).

But who am I to write a book telling you how to do this?

Well, for the past 6 years I've been a "community manager" by day and for the last 5 years I've been a "comedian" by night. A community manager is the not so fancy title they give people who manage online communities. A comedian is an equally not very fancy name they give people who tell jokes to strangers on stage.

In my day job I've managed large groups of people, written jokes for the web and made content that has helped grow the online communities of household brands including Marmite, Haribo, Pot Noodle, Carphone Warehouse, Tesco... I could go on but I think I've made my point.

I've a particular knowledge base and set of skills which has worked for brands all over the world. Now I've taken those skills and applied them to my career as a comedian. Slowly but surely I'm building my fan base of people who enjoy my work. And as I do that, I'm documenting and learning why and how connections grow online.

What you have in your hand is the result of reading obsessively about human behavior, online community building, memory techniques, what is needed to find your audience and more! In my experiments in social media I've made gigantic fuck ups that have ruined advertising campaigns and built fan bases which top a million members.

I've done it all so you don't have to. But you will.

Finding your feet in social media is a trial and error process but this book intends to cushion the blow you will inevitability feel something goes wrong, and help you know how to start and continue momentum when you begin to gain fans.

This book was funded through people who enjoy my work. It is living proof of the stuff within it. I was offered a publishing deal and turned it down because I thought it would be more fun (aka stress) to release it this way. The people this has been advertised to have discovered me through free content I created with love and put online.

Finally, please don't steal this book. I have decided to release it DRM free on my website because I want you to be able to put it on all your devices easily. By sending it to a friend you are losing me money. And I give enough away for free that the few things I charge for I need to keep cheap. The only way of doing that is if everyone buys a copy. And besides, we are all artists, so we need to stick together.

Chapter 1: How to make money out of your creativity?
From the Middle Ages to Renaissance Europe to the current day. I give you a brief history of how artists made money to continue creating what they do best.

Chapter 2: Aims.
What do you want to achieve? You can't achieve an aim without having a final goal in mind. Here's where you need to be honest with yourself about what you want so you can focus on how you're going to get it.

Chapter 3: Where are you at the moment?
You could be below the radar or have a growing fan base. You could even have a large fan base but not know how to make money from it. This is the chapter where we look at where you are in relation to your goal and how you can realistically achieve it using The Curve.

Chapter 4: How do you build and maintain an audience?
What do you need in order to attract an audience? And more importantly, what do you need to do to maintain it. In this chapter we look at how relationships between artists and fans develops online and start to reframe the idea of "Free" as a good thing.

Chapter 5: Why you shouldn't aim for the mainstream.
In this chapter we'll look at why "breaking the mould" or doing something unique is a great thing and you shouldn't fear it. The mainstream is dying and niche interest communities are growing as we'll see in the Long Tail Theory. By being specific in what you do you stand the greatest chance of attracting a loyal fan base.

Chapter 6: How many fans do you really need?
Do you really need a million fans to be profitable? Probably not. The number is probably closer to 1,000. In this chapter we'll look at how you find your True Fans and ask them (nicely) to support you.

Chapter 7: How can you be unique in your field?
Now that we've established why being unique is a good thing, we'll need to work out what's unique about you and why that's a really good and exciting thing. Oh there'll be **Purple Cows**.

Chapter 8: Why advertising undervalues content.
Can you live off internet adverts? Probably not. (Sorry to burst your bubble). Advertising can make you a bit of cash, but in this chapter we'll look into why that cash is short term, can lose you fans and ultimately devalues what you're trying to do.

Chapter 9: How to think like a fan.
Artists often forget that they're fans of someone else - usually the person who got them interested in the thing they're doing / making. Remembering how excited you are about another artist's work helps you get in the mindset of your fans which is important when it comes to building a relationship with them.

Chapter 10: Pick yourself.
Why you should be independent and not wait to make the thing you've always wanted. If it's good enough and finds a large enough audience the mainstream industry will beat a path to your door - by which time, you might not even need them.

Chapter 11: Why paywalls are the worst thing online.
Given that we established in Chapter 10 that giving away content is actually the first step in building a relationship, we look at paywalls and why these are not going to help you to continue to attract a wider and wider audience.

Chapter 12: Vanity Figures.
Numbers are fun online. From your Follower count on Twitter to your Fans on Facebook, it's easy to forget these numbers are people. They might make you feel good when they're going up, but they're vanity metrics and should be taken with a pinch of salt. What numbers matter and what numbers make us feel good aren't always the same thing.

Chapter 13: A Quick Guide to Crowdfunding.
In this chapter we'll deep dive into several methods of crowdfunding your art from the one-off method to the on-going financial support of your fans which can be so critical for artists.

Chapter 14: First Steps / Devising Own Targets.
Where do I go from here?

Now that you've learned everything I have to offer I will give you some final tips specific to your artistic field and also go into deep detail on what you can do to cultivate your community.

CHAPTER 1
How to make money out of your creativity.

Most artists focus on the "show" side of "show business". They put all their energy into building, creating and developing something that they're proud of. This is not a bad thing. But at the end of the creation process most artists do not know how to sell or market what they've made. But for an independent artist making something is only half your job. The other half is selling and marketing what you've made.

Some people think the secret to making money from online content is ad revenue, but as someone who has worked with advertisers I can tell you **ad revenue doesn't pay off** – even when you have a million hits.

In this book I take all my knowledge and research from the past 6 years of working in social media and distil it into only what you (an independent artist) need to know about -

- How to build an audience using the internet for your work.
- Why you don't need a million fans to be famous or profitable.
- How to sell and market digital content.
- Why you are your own best asset.
- How advertising devalues your content.

- Why giving away your work for free is a very good thing.
- How to minimise the online pirates.
- Why paywalls are the worst thing online.
- How a free view / hit / download doesn't equal a lost sale.
- Why average figures and stats online are never accurate.
- And finally why there's never been a better or easier time to do something you love and find an audience who will appreciate it.

But before we get into any of that we need to look at how artists made money before the internet and what we can learn from that process…

A brief history of marketing.

From the Middle Ages to Renaissance Europe.

The first way an artist would get funding to create some art is to be paid by someone who liked what they did. Arts patronage arose in countries all over Europe where a royal family, aristocracy or churches dominated a society and controlled the majority of the wealth.

As patrons the wealthier members of a society acted as sponsors to artists and commissioned artwork from individuals they liked. This system allowed artists to continue creating work without the need to sell physical copies of the work to a mass market. Painters often only created one version of a painting for a patron instead of today when they often need to sell 1,000s of copies in order to stay out of debt.

Case Study.

Mozart was funded by several wealthy businessmen during his life to continue to create music. His whole life he was a freelancer depending on less than a handful of people at any one time. He was once trying to raise money for a project and offered his backers their name in the program - like a very early version of crowdfunding.

During the Renaissance the church, Royal families and wealthy businessmen patronised many works of art, as this was the norm. We can date European patronage back to the Middle Ages.

Without arts patronage we wouldn't have had some of the work from famous artists including Leonardo da Vinci, Michelangelo, Ben Jonson and William Shakespeare.

Case Study.
Leonardo da Vinci depended on patrons throughout his life all of whom were very wealthy and powerful (including the King of France). Ludovico Maria Sforza was Duke of Milan from 1489 until 1500. He was also one of da Vinci's patrons and commissioned The Last Supper painting - one of the world's most famous paintings, and one of the most studied, scrutinized, and satirized. Without this one fan this painting would never have come into being.

A modern day equivalent to this would be an arts council grant. Sadly, these are near impossible to come by in the UK for an individual artists.

From around 1900 – 2000(ish) AD.
During this time period companies were developing digital recording methods and experimenting with different formats. Distribution was limited and a very expensive option for these physical products. However as the technology developed and improved the cost dropped and by the latter part of the 20th century it was possible for an individual artist to make their art, put it onto a physical artefact and sell it to an individual Fan.

Case Study.
Rock band Enter Shikari recorded their first three EPs and sold them at gigs with great success. This fan base was limited to people they could physically meet. After

a few years they began to put their music online to be streamed by potential fans which resulted in them gaining a global audience.

They continued this strategy for a few years and when they self published their first album it got to number 4 in the UK charts.

Just a thought...
How many bands have you purchased the album of without hearing the music first? Compare that to the number of bands you've purchased the album of when you've been given a preview / sample of the songs (this could have been online through YouTube, MySpace or Spotify or further back on TV programs like Top Of The Tops or radio charts). By sharing your work independently you're just extending the TV / Radio model but you have more control over where it goes and the quality in which it is consumed.

When compared to the patronage system you can see why this method is a much harder way for artists to make a living.

First of all it's based around scale. If you have a patron your funding is secured before you even begin making your art. If you're selling individual copies you need to sell a certain number of your art or products to be profitable. In order to sell enough copies you were highly dependant on advertising to get the largest number of people to know about your artwork.

With limited and expensive advertising options including a handful of terrestrial TV channels and a dozen radio stations, you needed to pay large sums of money to get your advert played and seen. As a result it was important to pick carefully where you advertised in order to make the most of your advertising budget. The TV and radio channels acted as the "gatekeeper" to whether your advert would get seen by the mass market or not.

To help pick where you advertised you would come up with a "target demographic / user". This would often be as vague as "mid-20s male living and working in the city of London" or as specific as "men aged between 20 and 30-year-old who enjoy jazz music". You might run focus groups or test adverts to see who was interested but ultimately you'd look at who is buying similar products in the market to work out who was most likely to buy your art.

By the end of the process your target audience is so vague it fits a large number of people who would be interested as well as lots who are not. Often products would be targeting an "average consumer" who didn't even exist.

You would buy advertising slots on TV or radio and interrupt a mass of people enjoying a program to tell them about what you have to offer in order to try and get more product awareness in the hope this would lead to sales (why this no longer works is covered in much more detail in **Chapter 7: How can you be unique in your field?**).

As the number of TV channels and radio stations went up the amount of programmes being broadcast also increased, allowing for advertisers to spread their budgets across a wider range of audiences who might be interested in buying what they have for sale.

TV channels and radio stations needed advertisers to stay in business so they had to pick and choose the programmes that would sell the most adverts but permitted creative freedom to attract the biggest audiences. TV companies knew this method of product-awareness advertising worked because before the internet content was scarce and peoples attention was valued highly by advertisers.

Key Point.
You don't know who is going to want to be in your audience.

You can try and target your audience but ultimately there will be anomalies. Comedian Andrew Whatts took a show up to the Edinburgh Fringe in 2014 called "Feminism For Chaps". He opened the show by explaining "if you're a woman in the audience, you already know all of this. I have nothing for you." Despite this, they stayed, kept coming and LOVED it. The show was highly praised and reviewed and was even given extra show dates.

His comment (although comical) would never be accurate.

I used to think my demographic for comedy was students. But a lot of my followers on Twitter are over 30 years old and in a career. When you're dealing with a potentially global audience, you're bound to attract people who don't fit into what you perceive to be "your audience" so don't think about "targeting" because if what you do is good, the people who are interested will come running.

The Age Of The Internet

The "dial-up" generation.
The Internet is a free (or very low cost) distribution network that is open to everyone. An artist doesn't need to convince a TV channel or radio station to showcase their work. You can put it up online for anyone to enjoy. This low barrier to entry allows artists to create and share their art faster and cheaper than ever.

Production costs have also dropped as a result of global online marketplaces like eBay. A musician can buy a secondhand guitar on eBay for £20 and a camera for £10, then search online for a free tutorial and teach themselves. After a few hours of practice you can record yourself covering a song and have it online for the world to see.

The problem with such low barriers to entry is that it has bred a large amount of creators and an ever-expanding list of niche interests. This abundance of content has caused artists to share what they do for free to build an audience rather than asking for money upfront for what they do. This has gradually caused "free" to become a common price point for most artists work.

High speed internet is introduced (where we are today).
We live in an age where you cannot easily make money by selling what you create. Content is infinitely copyable, effortlessly shareable and available for free to the entire world.

Although the cost of consuming content has dropped to almost nothing or free, the value of that art has stayed the same or increased. People are able to connect with artists on a personal level and build long-term relationships easier and faster than ever before.

Case Study.

Dodie Clark (known as Doddleoddle on YouTube[1]) started posting original music and covers in 2011. She grew her fan base by talking to people in the comments of her videos as well as the videos of YouTube musicians she enjoys. Since starting she's collaborated with massive YouTube stars including Tessa Violet, Hazel Hayes and Evan Edinger all of whom have over half a million subscribers.

She's started a "side channel" for more personal videos which have helped her develop deeper and stronger relationships with her fans. Sharing tour / gig diary entries and how she is feeling about her increasing fame.

Using her YouTube analytics she found out which city most of her subscribers lived and organised gigs in intimate venues. Almost all of which sold out.

She has no record label or management. What she does have is an audience globally who, if they can't make it down to gigs, can support her through regular donations in exchange for more free videos or they can buy merchandise including CDs and t-shirts.

We are quickly going back to a world where sponsoring artists or becoming a patron of somebodies work is commonplace and the norm. The difference is it's not the rich and wealthy individuals who are paying artists to keep creating; it's the general public.

Case Study.

Animator Yotam Perel puts up his cartoons to YouTube for free [2]. They've always been free and always will be. He has an audience of 136,000 subscribers. Instead of putting adverts on his work he asked them to donate some money towards the running of the project (if they wanted to). 144 of his Super Fans now give him $463.56 per animation. This gives him a budget and a wage to continue making his work.

If Yotam makes 4 animations per month he is earning $1854.24 per month. That's $22,250.88 per year.

His Super Fans aren't royalty or mega wealthy businessmen, they're people who appreciate his work. Work they would have never had a chance to see or enjoy if he hadn't shared it online for free.

144 people represents 0.11% of his YouTube audience. And at any point another fan might decide they want to give him some money to keep making the animations they love.

The power has shifted from the elite rich in society who sponsored 1 artist a lot of money to the general public who donate varying amounts to a selection of artists whose work they value. This method of making money can be split into two categories -

1. Patronage.
2. Crowdfunding.

Crowdfunding is where an artist asks for money to help them produce a project in exchange for gifts instead of ownership of the final product. These gifts vary but the general rule is the more money you give towards a project the more you get in return as a backer.

The main difference between patronage and crowdfunding is that patronage is ongoing sponsorship for regular work. Crowdfunding is collecting a specific amount of money over and above this for a bigger project.

An example of patronage would be fans sponsoring an artist per piece of online content they provide - even though that content is uploaded and shared for free to them and everyone else.

Patronage is different from a subscription model because in a subscription model the only variables are the number of people using the service and the number of paying users. To earn more they need more converts to pay. Patrons (Super Fans) can give whatever they want. Often this offsets the casual fans because they're not restricted to donating a set price for the work the artist creates.

Although the subscription model makes it easier to predict revenues and future profits it's a narrow way of looking at your fans. It puts them all in a one-size-fits-all box and assumes they all value your work the same.

An example of crowdfunding would be fans pre-ordering an album or DVD from an artist so the performer could afford to create the final product. The final product might then get released to the rest of the world for free.

In this book we'll look at the methods artists use to make money when everything can be found or consumed for free. We will see how "free" isn't a negative and can be the first step to attracting an audience for what you do. We will look at why you don't need millions of fans and the backing of a major corporation to be known.

There are several methods outlined in this book. You should pick the best few which suit you, your audience and your art. Some methods rely on the crowd funding approach and get your biggest supporters to pay for the work they value. Other methods focus on building relationships with your audience to create more of the things they love in the logic they'll buy merch from you later on. Combining methods gives you more revenue streams and decentralizes the money to make sure if one person can no longer support you, you're not left with no one to keep you afloat.

Ultimately this book is about helping you (an artist) to find an audience for your art and then showing you how to use the free online tools to connect with them and start to make money doing what you love.

To sum up...

- Most artists focus on the "show" side of "show business".
- Without arts patronage we wouldn't have had some of the work from famous artists including Leonardo da Vinci, Michelangelo, Ben Jonson and William Shakespeare. A modern day equivalent to this would be an arts council grant.
- You don't know who is going to want to be in your audience.
- The problem with such low barriers to entry is that it has bred a large amount of creators and an ever-expanding list of niche interests.
- Although the cost of consuming content has dropped to almost nothing or free, the value of that art has stayed the same or increased.

CHAPTER 2
Aims.

What do you want to achieve?

Before we begin I should say these are just guidelines and not strict "must do's". The marketplace doesn't always behave in real life quite as neatly as it does in a book, and your fans may be exactly the sort of free thinkers who like to buck trends. There's practical advice and case studies but mostly the knowledge is what you should know but you do not have to know all of it. Some performers use free content to gain a live offline audience and that's enough. Some online video creators use their audience to get a wage to keep creating free content. It all depends on the individual artist.

You should have a clear aim for what you want before you begin your strategy. You should be as specific as you can. For me:

I am a comedian.

From my audience I want to tour a new hour-long show every year to a good-sized crowd (50-100 people) 100 nights of the year. I also want to write my own projects like online content (sketches etc) and write books on marketing and social media.

Now it's your turn:

I am a _____

From my audience I want

_____

CHAPTER 3
Where are you at the moment?

You might have been playing music for years, but only in your bedroom. Or you might be a comedian who has been going round and round the circuit for over a decade. This isn't what I am talking about. I am referring to where are you in terms of generating your own audience.

Growing your audience will always be part of your work but depending on what stage you're at will inform your next move towards the goal you just outlined.

Here are some rough categories, you should slide into one easily or be between two.

1. **Under The Radar** – at this stage you'll be trying to make yourself stand out from the pack. You'll have no audience and even struggle to get friends and family to come watch you. At this stage you should be working on your art.
2. **First Noticed** – at this stage you'll have elevated yourself from the pack. You'll have something about yourself and your work which people will be talking about but you'll still only have a core small group of fans. You should invest in these people as they invested in you early.
3. **Hot & New** - at this stage you'll have a base of Super Fans who rave about what you do as well as some more casual fans who enjoy what you do, but barely spread the word about it. You might even get the odd bit of press coverage.

4. **Peak of Potential** – at this stage you'll be getting a large amount of exposure equal or in line with the potential growth of your audience. You should continue to invest in the Super Fans who found you earlier in your career as well as talk and build on the relationships you have with your new fans. This is key as if you ignore a fan or ruin a potential relationship it's much harder to get that person back into your audience.
5. **Cult / Infamous** - at this stage you'll have a group of fans who are highly dedicated to you and your work. You'll also have casual fans but most of your audience will be die hard lovers of what you do. You should continue to give back to these people as they'll always be with you.
6. **Star** - at this stage you're famous. Maybe even a household name. People will know who you are and some of what you do - even people who don't like you. At this stage you'll need a thick skin to ignore the people who'd rather not know you even exist. The best way of dealing with this stage is to focus on the core of your audience.
7. **Legend** - you've been around long enough that you're no longer just working on what you do, but the things you do are starting to turn into a legacy.
8. **Retired** - you've had your 15 minutes of fame and now you've still got your core fans, but your level of fame and popularity has started to decline or end completely.

To estimate this (and see what size audience you should realistically expect) you need to know about *The Curve [1]*.

The Curve is a business model that focuses on building a connection with individual people and letting them spend varying amounts of money on products, services and experiences they value.

The Curve comes in three parts –

1. Using Free Content to find and build an audience.
2. Using technology to figure out what that audience values and to move them along the Curve from Freeloaders to Super Fans.
3. Using a selection of price points to allow your Super Fans to spend lots of money on things they value.

Finding an audience has always been a challenge to an artist. If nobody knows what you do, how are they going to know if they want or need it in their lives?

Your Fans are able to get your work for free legally or illegally so by sharing it directly with the world you're able to take control over what's available and the quality at which they see your art.

"Free" is a bit of a buzzword that can make artists worry. The reason it makes artists worry is because they've looked at how big corporations sales have been hit by internet piracy and believe the news media's conclusion that putting something online for free means you lost a sale.

The Curve looks at it another way. We see sharing free content as the starting point in a relationship with a potential fan and not a lost sale.
People buy from people they trust.

The quicker you lose your fear of "free" content the faster you'll start to connect and discover an audience for your work.

How many times have you purchased something from an artist without knowing anything about what they do? Unless a close friend made a recommendation my guess is never.

Case Studies.
Musician Alex Day - Gave away a torrent of his music (along with music videos on YouTube and streams on Spotify) so people could hear the songs before buying.

He gained an audience of over 1 million subscribers on YouTube. He used this audience to become the Guinness World Record holder for the highest-charting single by an unsigned artist. As well as getting 3 singles into the top 40 charts.

Writer Tim Ferriss - Gave away large chunks of his book (both in audio and written format) for free so people could see what it was about before buying. He also offered more content in a "premium" bundle in exchange for the person's email address [2].

All three of Tim's books made it into the New York Times best-sellers list.

If people enjoy an artist's work some will support it. It won't be all of them, but you don't need them all. In the past, an artist had to appeal to a lot of people in their local area. Now, an artist's audience can be small in number but global in reach.

If 100 people downloaded Alex or Tim's bundles. Maybe 50 of them enjoyed the content. Maybe 25 liked it enough to pay for it, the others didn't want to, but told a friend (who might buy it). Of those 25 who liked it enough to pay for it, maybe 10 (at best) had the money in their bank (and the time coming up in their lives) to invest in purchasing the product from them. The rest might come back to it at pay day or forget about it completely.

A free download doesn't equal a lost sale.

Some of the 50 downloads might have loved a copy of their work but not had the money right away. Others might have enjoyed it but not felt it was worth the amount it was on sale for and so would never purchase it anyway.

An offline example of this is when you go up to a food sampling table in a supermarket. Chances are you won't like the food, but because it's free, you give it a go. Even if you do like it, the chances are you won't buy it then and there. However next time you have a bit of spare money and fancy a change which product are you going to pick... one you've tried and know you like. Or one you might have to buy a whole pack of and hate the taste?

But it doesn't have to be free. Free is the ideal in The Curve but a low price point also works for artists. Many American performers have made digital downloads of their shows available for $5 while still charging $30 or more for tickets to the live shows.

When you make music in the Internet age your songs need to be made available for free on YouTube or Spotify as a preview for things they can purchase like CDs, DVDs or tickets to live shows. Some people will buy it, but ultimately the majority of listeners will be consuming it for free. To look at a YouTube video of your music and say "a million people watched it, but I only sold 1,000 albums" is the wrong attitude. It is based on an arrogant way of looking at each view: like everyone valued the work in the same way and that value was 'this is the best album of all time I better buy it', which is clearly not the case. You sold 1,000 albums… that's amazing.

Free content is not the enemy to your profitability. It's your competition building better relationships with their fans or audience. It's why some Fans will spend £200 on a limited edition version of a CD they can buy for £10. They feel connected with the creator and as a result want to support them.

To understand why the majority of the world won't spend money on what you do we need to look at the globe as one big marketplace.

The Curve shows that the majority of the world will not pay for what you do, but we know this doesn't matter, as all you need to find is around 1,000 True Fans out of the 7,000,000,000 people living on Earth.

With the mass markets narrowing or coming to an end, the world of niche interests is fast becoming the norm. Focusing on your audience is much more important than what the rest of the world is doing. It's not a competition; it's about doing something remarkable and interesting.

Case and point

Sixto Diaz Rodriguez, also known as Rodríguez or Jesús Rodríguez is an American folk singer who made little to no money or impact in the USA but his albums became both successful and influential in South Africa where his record sales outnumbered Elvis [3]. How he was so unknown in his home country of America but gained notoriety and fame in South Africa (even though very little was known about him in that country was explored in detail in the film "Searching for Sugarman") [4].

Imagine everyone in the world is standing in a line on a graph's X axis (diagram below).

On the **left hand side** are your **True Fans**, the backbone of your earnings who will pay several times the price for an album than the casual fan because it's a limited edition. This is your **revenue opportunity**.

Like the person who has every Beatles album in mono and stereo, on vinyl, CD and MP3. The Beatles haven't produced a new song since 1970 yet they are still selling records, mostly to people who already own them.

On the **right hand side** you have people **who don't like what you do** and wouldn't pay for it. Alternatively they don't know what you do and have yet to hear about your work. This is your **marketing opportunity**.

Now imagine each person has a line coming out of the top of their head showing how much they'd be willing to spend on you in an average year (y axis below). It might look something like this -

x-axis: Every person in the world, ranked by the amount they are prepared to spend with you
y-axis: Amount a person is prepared to spend with you

By offering people free content at the tail end (right side) of The Curve you give the billions of people who don't know what you do a chance to sample it and grow as a fan.

Offering several price points or even "pay what you think it is worth" you give fans the freedom to give whatever they feel comfortable with.

By putting up a paywall you're restricting the number of people who can discover you.
(We will discuss this in more detail later in the book in **Chapter 11: Why paywalls are the worst thing online.**)

Case Studies.
Julia Nunes funded an album with the help of just 1,685 of her fans ($77,888). That's an average donation of $46.22 per backer. [5]

Amanda Palmer funded her EP with just 437 fans ($8,581). That's an average of $19.63 per backer. [6]

Alan Becker funded his short animation film (Animator vs Animation IV) with just 446 fans ($11,280). That's an average of $25.29 per backer. [7]

All of these people made significant sums of money from their Super Fans which they acquired by giving away content for free to build an audience for what they want to do and also proving they're not only able to do it, but are the only people you can find doing it in the way they do.

By allowing an ongoing relationship with someone in your audience you keep the door open for someone to help fund a project in the future. You never know who will be your biggest spending fan.

In the film Pretty Woman, Vivian Ward (played by Julia Roberts) goes into a shop where the sales staff snap judge her as someone who cannot afford the clothing. They treat her poorly and she leaves. The next day (after spending what looks like thousands of dollars on clothing) she storms into the shop and asks the sales assistant if she works on commission. When she confirms that she does, Vivian holds up the 20 bags of branded clothings she's holding and yells "Big Mistake!" and storms out.

You never know who your biggest fan is going to be.

Case Studies.

When online cartoon Cyanide & Happiness did their KickStarter they offered 1 fan to "fly with a friend (within US) to Dallas for the Banana Bar Crawl (April 13, 2013) and put you in a hotel near the event. You will be given a banana costume, a crown, scepter and "royal throne". Your personal assistant will announce you at every bar and take care of your drinks. And a surprise or two." for $10,000. And 1 person purchased it. This Super Fan loves their work and will pay a premium to spend time with the artist and support their future creations.

If you think of the freeloaders (right side of The Curve) as potential converts / fans you stop seeing them as freeloaders costing you money with nothing in return, you see them as a targeted **marketing opportunity** that can seek you out.

Remember: Every Super Fan was once a freeloader.

Variable price points are when you give fans multiple levels at which they can financially support you. This is giving your fans total freedom to show you how much they value your work. Because art touches everybody in a different way you can never be 100% sure what every person values your work at. It could be nothing, or it might be much more than you would ever think a single person would pay for it.

Fans of your music might want to give you £50 for an album even though they're used to spending £10 in shops because they feel a connection with you and know how much time and effort you've put into making the free content they've enjoyed.

> **The internet has made variable prices for products and merchandise a lot easier for both the artist and the fan.**

Case Studies.
The makers of the Pebble watch found 68,929 backers and raised $10,266,845 to put their watch into production.

Within that funding they were able to offer fans the option of giving the company $1. In exchange for their $1 the backer gets "Exclusive updates on the products development" aka a monthly newsletter. The sort that most people consider annoying and send to trash without reading... and 2,615 people did it! Later in the book we discuss the difference between "permission" and "interrupt" marketing which explains why people would pay to sign up for a newsletter. [8]

Comedian Ron Lechler made a documentary about his experiences of being a stand up at "the bottom rung" of the ladder. He raised $1,084 through 37 backers.

2 people gave $1 in exchange for a "Facebook and Twitter thanks".
4 people gave $5 in exchange for a thank you in the films credits.
2 people gave $5 and in exchange "Ron will write your name on a piece of paper and give it to a stranger".
The list goes on and on. [8]

If you have a good idea, take it to the crowd and let the free market do the rest. The reason big corporations are doing badly (or worse than they used to) is that because they're still marketing to everyone in the world (which costs a lot of money) as they don't know who will be interested. These ideas tend to be unadventurous and boring. Big corporations fear "free" because they've never had to market products this way. Faceless corporations struggle because people buy from people, and the opposite of a trustworthy human that you've made a strong connection with is a faceless big business.

Variable pricing and the pay-what-you-want model works better for artists as opposed to businesses because you (the artist) have a much more personal and individual relationship with the buyer / backer. As an artist you're a person who can be contacted through social media, email or in real life. If you want to contact a business you'll need to ring a helpline or go into a store where you'll talk to any number of staff that aren't always interested in helping nurture a one-to-one connection with you (the buyer / backer) and the business you're buying from.

You're selling your merchandise on a much more personal and emotional level. As a result, sometimes logical pricing goes out of the window.

Think about auction houses and how rare, limited edition or one off pieces of art go for large sums of money. A painting is only worth what someone will pay for it, and at some point the level of "skill" you have is not as big of a factor as who you are to the fan.

Fixed pricing has the problem that an artist has to estimate what people will pay for it. An artist is clearly biased about their work. When you're good at creating something (poetry, films, music etc) you don't see the value in it in the same way a lot of other people who don't have those talents will. The fans should always be deciding what your work is worth and online it is cost-effective to allow them to do so.

Having a fixed price for your products limits your Super Fans. They might want to give you a hundred times as much as a casual Fan for your work.

Someone who has just discovered your work will value it a lot less than a Super Fan who has been following your career for years.

When they put millions of dollars into a production, the backers of plays and musicals are in effect buying the most expensive theatre tickets in the world. Why not wait until the show comes out and get a front row seat at a thousandth of the price? **Because if they didn't there would be no art.**

Case Studies.

Every year I organise a mass online collection for a homeless shelter using various online forums I admin. I ask everyone (if they can afford it) to donate £1. Last year one person anonymously donated £200. We raised a little over £1,100. This person lives in one of my online forums, but I have no idea who it is. But I know they're there. [9]

If I had set the donation button at £1 the person who gave me £200 would have been limited and the charity would have lost £199.

Musician Jack Conti is crowdsourcing funds for his upcoming music videos through Patreon. He's asked his audience to give what they want at the different levels he's set. If he had said "can everyone give me £1" he would be losing most of his funding as only 570 of his 1,400 backers give him $1. [10]

461 give him $3.
137 give him $5.
142 give him $10.
3 give him $100.

Total - $3,788

If he had limited his fans to $5 per video he would have potentially lost 461 $3 fans who might not want to (or be able to) give him $5. That would have lost him $1389.

If we assume all the fans donating above $5 would give him $5 instead of $10 or $100 he would get more $5 donations but lose money.

*He would get **282 $5** donations totaling **$1,410**.*

Currently his $5 or higher donors are giving him a total of $2,405.

So he would lose $995 simply because his biggest fans were not given the option of supporting him to the extent they want to.

The Curve is different from the Freemium model.

Freemium: a free product, normally either a limited version of the full product or a full version of the product but with a time restriction on it.

In the Freemium pricing strategy you put a product online for free (this would normally either be a limited version of the full product or a full version of the product but with a time restriction on it). This would attract interest from people who might want to purchase the full version. If the person trying out the product enjoys it they can pay a fixed price amount to buy it.

Examples of Freemium products include apps which make you pay to remove adverts and cloud server hosting which give you the first XX Gbs for free and then charge you a fee for additional space.

In the case of giving someone a limited version of the product with a fixed price you're limiting your Super Fans who might want to pay you more than your asking price.

In the case of the time-limited demo you're forcing someone to make a decision and then only offering them a single price point (which we already know to be a bad move). It's the offline equivalent of giving someone a sample of some food and then hanging out asking if they want to buy some more until they've finished their mouthful. Would this encourage you to buy?

The biggest criticism of the Freemium model is that it creates a large number of Freeloaders that can't be sustained by the small numbers of paying users.

You will get some customers through frustration (ie they don't want to click through the ads) but they won't feel any particular loyalty to your product or brand. This is the worst way to start a relationship with a fan / customer because you might get paid, but think of the "story" they'll tell their friends "it's a great product, but I felt forced into signing up because I didn't have an alternative".

The Curve shows how the Freemium model could work better: it's not because people aren't spending money on the product or services they value, it's because they're limited on how much they are able to support the things they love. Having a set price for the premium services stops the Super Fans from giving as much as they'd like. It also stops the casual Fans or Freeloaders from giving £1 here and there, which helps towards the overall revenue.

Case Studies.

The Comedy Button is a website that produces free weekly podcasts and videos. They have asked their fans if they value their work enough to donate what they think it is worth to keep the site going. 4979 people (backers) now donate $18,659 per month. The Comedy Button offers 11 levels of payment ranging from $1 for a thank you on the website (1855 backers) to $100,000 for "anything you want" (0 backers). [11]

Total

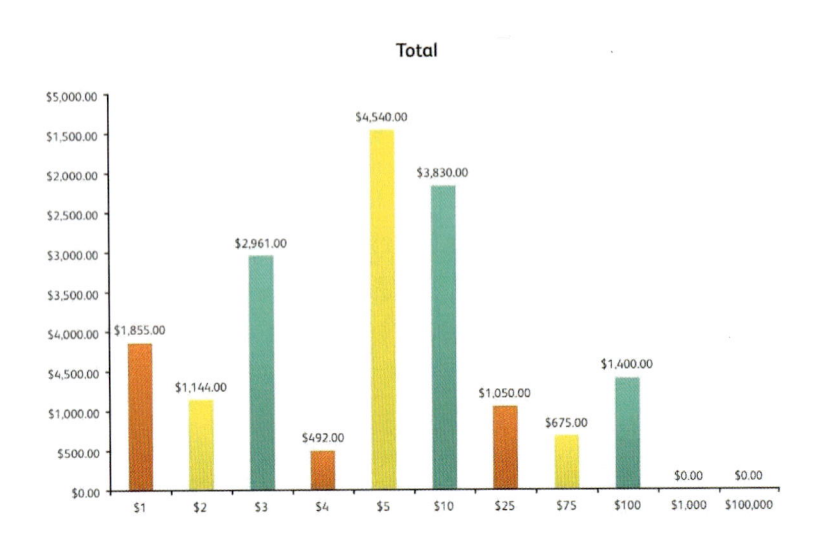

Price	Amount
$1	$1,855.00
$2	$1,144.00
$3	$2,961.00
$4	$492.00
$5	$4,540.00
$10	$3,830.00
$25	$1,050.00
$75	$675.00
$100	$1,400.00
$1,000	$0.00
$100,000	$0.00

Most of their money comes from the 908 $5 backers.

If they'd only offered the $5 price point (and we ignore the fact that some of the $5 backers might have been put off by the fact it was the only price option) The Comedy Button would be losing out on all the donations from the 3,537 people who give between $1-4. That's $6,452 per month, which is $1912 more than the $5 price point.

Now let us assume the people who give more than $5 would still give money but only $5 as that's all they'd allowed to contribute. The Comedy Buttons revenue would go from $6,955 to $2,240. A loss of $4,715, which is $175 more than the $5 donors.

You might listen to The Comedy Button and think it's not worth $75 or $100 a month. But 23 people do. And you are all correct.

The most valuable thing about art is the creation process and the final product. The final product should be a one off, but thanks to the Internet digital versions can be shared and copied infinitely at very little cost. However the value is still in the scarce number of copies of the original product that cannot easily be replicated.

Digital music is replicable and as such is what musicians should be giving away for free as a sample of what they create. Live shows are at a premium as there'll never be an abundance of them because the artist is limited to how many performances they can do in a lifetime.

The best way to tell what's at a premium is by thinking how scarce they are (or potentially are). Simply by answering the following questions should give you an idea how much to charge your audience for it (from free to very expensive).

1. How many of the thing do you have?
2. How many can you produce if demand for it went up?
3. Can the thing be made digitally without losing any value in the thing?

To give you an example:

Example 1 - Live shows.

1. **How many of the thing do you have?**
   I've 20 live dates booked in the next 3 months.
2. **How many can you produce if demand for it went up?**
   I could do another 10-15. So in total I could have a max of 35 per 3 months.
3. **Can the thing be made digitally without losing any value in the thing?**
   No. (Live recordings are a different thing as we'll see in a minute).

As I can only produce 35 shows in 3 months this thing is scarce and so should be at a premium.

Example 1 - Live recording of a show.

1. **How many of the thing do you have?**
   I've a digital file so unlimited.
2. **How many can you produce if demand for it went up?**
   I can make an unlimited number of copies.
3. **Can the thing be made digitally without losing any value in the thing?**
   Yes. If anything selling a DVD as a digital file makes it easier to distribute and sell to my fans.

As I can produce an unlimited number of DVDs (or digital files) very quickly this item is in abundance and so should be available for free and at a low price point to my fans.

The Curve is about finding an audience, developing a relationship with them and then finding a cost-effective way to allow your Fans to support you at a price point that suits them. This might be nothing or this might be much higher than you would ever price your own work.

To sum up…

- Growing your audience will always be part of your work but depending on what stage you're at will inform your next move towards the goal you just outline.
- The Curve looks at it another way. We see sharing free content as the starting point in a relation with a potential fan and not a lost sale. People buy from people they trust.
- The quicker you lose your fear of "free" content the faster you'll start to connect and discover an audience for your work.
- Free content is not the enemy to your profitability. It's your competition building better relationships with their fans or audience.
- Offering several price points or even "pay what you think it is worth" you give fans the freedom to give whatever they feel comfortable with.
- By putting up a paywall you're restricting the number of people who can discover you.
- You never know who your biggest fan is going to be.
- Remember: Every Super Fan was once a freeloader.
- The internet has made variable prices for products and merchandise a lot easier for both the artist and the fan.
- You're selling your merchandise on a much more personal and emotional level. As a result, sometimes logical pricing goes out of the window.
- Having a fixed price for your products limits your Super Fans. They might want to give you a hundred times as much as a casual Fan for your work.
- The best way to tell what's at a premium is by thinking how scarce they are (or potentially are).

CHAPTER 4
How do you build and maintain an audience?

How to build an engaged audience.
Building an audience to support what you do can be split into three basic parts. You'll need to answer the questions at each stage before you can begin. Below is a template for how you can generally get started, where you go from there is up to you and your vision for your art and your audience.

Forget thinking about "free content" as an endpoint for your audience building activity. The conversation begins with free content. If it makes it easier, think of it as "sharing your work".

You have to begin with free content which gives onlookers and bystanders a reason to talk to you. Without examples of your work… how will they know you're worth investing in? After your work has caught their eye, you must keep providing high quality content. This slowly builds up connections and a relationship with the audience. You can then build on that relationship and move them along from being a Freeloader to a Fan and finally (for the elite few) a Super Fan.

You should always be asking yourself how many more people trust your content, art or words now than did 6 months ago. You should be constantly building a fanbase who increasingly value what you're doing. Even if this is 1 person every 6 months, that's still progress. The point is to always be as self-aware as possible about who your Fans and Super Fans are.

Brands are often worried about being too bold, out there or exciting. They play it safe to protect their "branding". Which is actually the worst thing they can do. Safe is boring. In the online world we can connect with anybody… so why would we want to connect with someone who is boring?

Be exciting, controversial, distinctive.

There are two things to remember when planning your content strategy:

1) If your art or content can be easily converted to a digital format this will be your free (or low) price point.
2) Your time is the most expensive and scarce commodity.

Free
How do you build an audience and get them to care about what you do?

As an artist, your free content is whatever you do that can be easily converted into a digital format and uploaded to the internet. If you're a comedian this could be a video of a live performance or throw away jokes on Twitter. If you're a musician this will be your songs on Spotify or music videos on YouTube. If you are a poet this would be your poems on a Tumblr or quotes from your work on image hosting sites.

Whatever you upload you need to make it as discoverable as possible and easy to share. This is how you start to attract and build an audience and in turn that audience shows their friends which helps grow your reach and potential audience numbers.

The things you offer can also be on sale at a low cost or pay-what-you-want model such as a song on iTunes for 79p or a DVD download for £5 but it's vitally important that you make it available for people to try for free.

Remember, if your art can be made digital it will most likely be shared somewhere online illegally at some point anyway. Don't turn potential Super Fans into guilt-ridden criminals.

This is not a lost sale this is a lost relationship.

There's very little evidence to support that a download would have been a sale. How many times have you listened to a track on Spotify and been thankful you didn't have to buy it before listening? The play count is meaningless. It always goes up and is a vanity metric. I've downloaded hundreds of mobile apps only to delete them a week or two later when I've lost interest. Most of these apps I'd never opened.

Free is more about being discoverable and is your online calling card. Share your work with the world and trust that a percentage of the audience for your art will pay for it down the road.

Be aware before you upload anything that by joining a social media site you're taking part in a community that already exists. You're adding your voice to the conversation and as such you should treat it as a longterm project.

Think about how you discovered the last artist online that you love. Did you have to pay to view their work? Or did you get the chance to browse it first? Would you have given them a second glance if you'd had to pay upfront? Be honest with your answers here and it'll guide you to make the best choices when it comes to what you give away to make your art discoverable.

Examples and ideas.
Before you think about uploading any content, make sure you pick the correct site to put it onto. There are lots of content sharing sites available and you want to

ignore the total number of users for now. When deciding which site to upload to think about -

- How will your content look on the platform?
- Is it the best place for it to be discovered? (Vimeo video uploads look better than YouTube, but YouTube is much more SEO friendly because they're owned by Google etc)
- Will you be able to maintain a community on that site should it take off?

Here are some examples for free content you can give away to help attract an audience.

Musicians

- Finished music can be made streamable on Last.fm, Spotify, SoundCloud and on your own site.
- Music you have written can be made free to download from your blog / website - and encourage people to try and do their own covers of your songs.
- Your "behind-the-scenes" or "making of" footage from the studio (even if that studio is in your bedroom) can be uploaded to YouTube.

Comedians

- Your joke ideas can be posted on Twitter.
- The audio of your jokes can be made into an album and uploaded to Spotify.

Actors / Directors / Movie Makers

- Behind-the-scenes footage (as long as it's not against any rules) can be uploaded to YouTube as part of an ongoing video blog.

- Your experiences in creating something (eg your first feature film) can be blogged on Tumblr so other filmmakers can learn from you and share advice.
- Blooper reels can be shared on video sharing sites.

Artists / illustrators

- Early sketches can be made available on image sharing sites.
- Do your own versions of other peoples work to show how you would have done it on photoshopping community sites like Dribbble.com

Make-Up Artists

- Product reviews to help novices understand when and how a product should be used. Showing you're knowledgeable makes you more of an authority and much more likely to be someone people trust when looking to hire.
- Make-up tutorials show you know what you're doing and if you also show where people go wrong, can save your audience both time and money.

Voice over artists

- Upload a showreel of what you've done in the past so people can get an idea of your talents.
- Make a podcast of your voices.

These are just a few ideas to get your mind thinking of content you can make or might already have which you can be sharing to become more discoverable. If you're still stuck for ideas, get a starting point by looking at people online you admire the work of for inspiration.

Middle ground
What do you need to do to move Freeloaders to Fans and then (for the elite few) to Super Fans?

These people like your work and want to support you, a bit. They're not Super Fans (yet) but they do enjoy your work enough to pay for it. These Fans understand how much money, time and effort you put into your art and know that you need to make money to keep creating.

The easiest thing to offer here is a low price point for what you gave away for free. If you put your music up for streaming on Spotify you can add the option for them to buy it for a very low fee. If you uploaded a live performance video you can offer people the chance to pay to download it. Even better, these Fans can gift it easily to their friends.

By offering loads of price points we know we can move a Fan along to spending more than they would if the spending brackets were further apart. So give them a lot of choice and remember: the more they spend, the more they should get back. This doesn't just mean offering them products you can offer them something that strengthens their relationship or connection with you. Offering a personal email "thanks" for being the first 100 people to download a single is an inexpensive way of adding value to a product and can help encourage someone to buy from you.

The key thing to remember when offering to sell a product to anyone online is to ensure you have as much control over the relationship with the Fan as you can. If you sell your products through Amazon or iTunes they're taking that data and using it to work out what those customers want. If you can sell it direct through your website or from a CrowdSourcing platform you're able to get more information about your Fans and what they want from you. I'm not saying you shouldn't use Amazon or iTunes, I am just saying be aware that the relationship with the individual Fan should always be a factor in all your choices.

Examples and ideas.

Musicians

- *You can offer your free music streams for a very low price via iTunes.*
- *You can crowdsource donations via PayPal for money towards your next music video.*
- *You can add value to your existing product line by signing CDs or handwriting thank you letters to the early buyers.*

Comedians

- *You can put your DVD / video of your set on a pay-what-you-want site.*
- *You can offer Fans the option to donate towards your costs for making free tweets / videos through Patreon or Paypal.*
- *You can add value to your products by offering to give a shout-out on social media or on your website to anyone who gives you more than £10 per month in support.*

Actors / Directors / Movie Makers

- *You can auction off tickets to the opening night of your show.*
- *You can ask for a small ongoing amount of financial support through PayPal or Patreon to pay you for your time.*
- *You can add value by exclusively selling a version of the DVD / show program to your mailing list with artwork only available to people who have joined your online community.*

Artists / illustrators

- *You can add value by offering a limited run of pictures at certain times of the year (Valentine's Day / Christmas etc).*
- *You can make your images available in different sizes digitally for a lower cost than it would be to buy it e.g. a desktop background image or a Facebook cover photo for 79p.*

Make-Up Artists

- *You can use affiliate links to products and ask your audience to click and buy through them so you get a cut but it doesn't cost them any more money.*
- *You can also sell an ebook of reviews with extra hints and tips themed around certain subjects such as halloween make-up, or "Saturday night out" make-up etc.*

Voice over artists

- *You can offer your audience the chance to suggest which voices you do / upload next and pay a small fee towards the production.*
- *You can record voicemail messages in character voices and send them to people over the internet.*

Start by thinking small. Look at what you already make and take it one step further. If you're struggling for ideas, put yourself in the mindset of someone in your audience. Think of someone you like online, what would you want from them? Then think of someone you adore the work of, what would you want from them? Offer both. You might not have anyone who feels a real connection with your work at the moment, but having the option gives them a chance to support you should they move towards becoming a Super Fan.

If you're still struggling for ideas, don't worry. In Chapter 11: How to think like a fan, we go into more detail on this which should help ease you into this process and help get your mind thinking about what you can do to add value to what you're already doing.

Expensive

How can you make it possible for your Super Fans to spend as much as they want on the things they value?

Your Super Fans are the backbone of your revenue as an independent artist. It is the smallest group of fans you have but they're the most valuable asset available to you. These people all value your work differently but share one fact: they all highly value what you do and are willing to pay an amount that reflects this. So give them the chance to do that.

It is worth noting, not all Super Fans will financially back you. Some Super Fans can't but go out of their way to help you promote a gig by telling friends you're coming to town, or share your work on their social media channels. These are still Super Fans.

Super Fans are the people who will buy limited edition CDs or signed merchandise. You're selling to people on an emotional level. They have a strong relationship with you or your art and as a result most of these products won't be digital.

These Super Fans are buying things for social value as well as the prestigious fact of owning the artefact or experience. They may have already purchased the digital download of your book but want the physical signed limited edition for the bragging rights.

Musicians can sell limited edition CDs, tour DVDs, signed t-shirts, B-side tracks that didn't make it to the CD, handwritten lyrics… the list goes on. Artists can sell custom drawings and one off original prints. You could even sell an evening with your biggest fans where they can go out for a meal with you or stand by the side of the stage at a show.

It is harder to give general examples in this area, because every artist's work and merchandise portfolio is unique - which gives you the opportunity to really get creative.

If you're stuck for ideas you can think of what you would buy from your heroes and then offer that or, even better, ask your audience what they want from you using social media.

Examples and ideas.

Musicians

- *Limited edition artwork CDs / DVDs.*
- *Handwritten lyrics.*
- *Google / Skype Hangouts to learn your songs.*

Comedians

- *DVD bonus features e.g. extra jokes / outtakes.*
- *Notes from your notebook.*
- *Pre-sale / priority sale tickets to your shows.*

Actors / Directors / Movie Makers

- *For people who donate a lot of money you can give them credits in the film or tickets to the premiere screening.*
- *Cameos in the film.*
- *Backstage access.*

Artists / illustrators

- *Really limited edition prints.*
- *Early sketches.*
- *Custom drawings.*

Make-Up Artists

- *Meeting face-to-face to do make-up.*
- *Skype / Google Hangout meeting to have a private lesson.*
- *Exclusive DVDs of tutorials.*
- *A box of limited edition products (if you make your own stuff).*

Voice over artists

- *You'll do a voiceover for them for a film / trailer / game.*
- *You'll teach them how to do accents.*

If you're stuck for inspiration you can either browse KickStarter for ideas or have a look at what the artists you adore are offering. Get in the mind of your audience. What do you think they'd want from you? Is there a video / blog post / update which did much better than everything else you've done which you can do more of?

The best way of getting into the mind of your audience is by asking them what they want from you. If you can provide it, give it to them, if you can't, make a list and check back on it regularly to see if you can work towards it in the future. This will also help you identify who are your Super Fans, who are your Fans and who is moving along from freeloader to Fan or Fan to Super Fan.

To sum up....

- Forget thinking about "free content" as an endpoint for your audience building activity. The conversation begins with free content. If it makes it easier, think of it as "sharing your work".
- You should always be asking yourself how many more people trust your content, art or words now than did 6 months ago.
- Safe is boring. In the online world we can connect with anybody... so why would we want to connect with someone who is boring?
- Remember, if your art can be made digital it will most likely be shared somewhere online illegally at some point anyway. Don't turn potential Super Fans into guilt-ridden criminals.
- This is not a lost sale this is a lost relationship.
- The easiest thing to offer here is a low price point for what you gave away for free.
- It is worth noting, not all Super Fans will financially back you. Some Super Fans can't but go out of their way to help you promote a gig by telling friends you're coming to town, or share your work on their social media channels. These are still Super Fans.
- Super Fans are the people who will buy limited edition CDs or signed merchandise. You're selling to people on an emotional level.

CHAPTER 5
Why you shouldn't aim for the mainstream.

The big reason you shouldn't aim for the mainstream is because these are the people who are being catered to and are good at not listening. People who have niche interests are hungry for content.

The Long Tail Theory is an economic model that shows how the "market" (aka everyone in the world's attention) has shifted away from focusing on mainstream products at the head of the demand curve **towards a massive, ever** widening number of niches at the tail (see figure 1) [1].

Figure 1

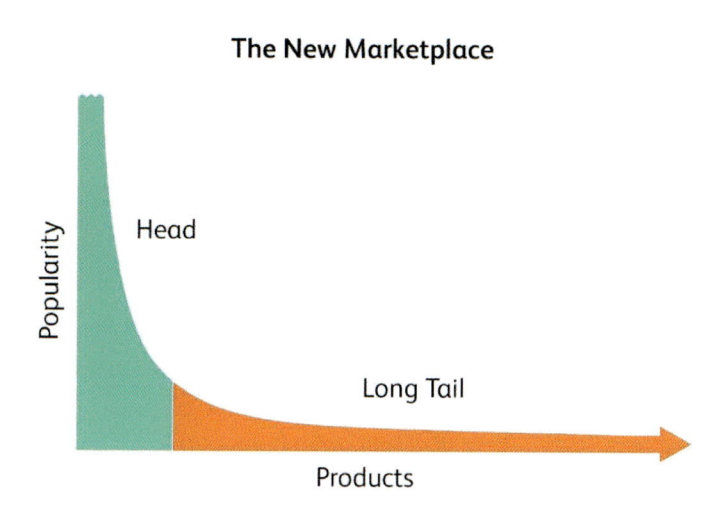

The New Marketplace

[Graph showing Popularity on y-axis and Products on x-axis. A green "Head" section on the left shows high popularity, transitioning into an orange "Long Tail" extending to the right.]

The big green section is full of the mainstream "*hits*" that have dominated the market and culture for a long time. These include books, films and albums from major record labels that make it into high-street shops and department stores.

The longer, ever expanding orange section is the "*non-hits*" which is full of niches and older products that used to be in the "*hits*".

Before online distribution existed (let alone got popular) people had to go to shops to purchase anything and everything. But shops can only stock a certain number of products due to the physical constraints. For the most part these products came from the mainstream publishers, as these were the lowest risk items that were most likely to sell to the mass market. This is why they're referred to as "hits".

If a shop wanted to stock more products they would have to increase the available shelf space, which isn't cheap to do in the physical world.

Online it costs next to nothing to list another 5,000 items for a retailer like Amazon.

Half of all books sold on Amazon aren't available in shops. They're self published works sold directly from the writer to the readers.

An online retailer's success is made or broken by the efficiency of their recommendation engine. NetFlix, iTunes, Amazon, Kindle and Spotify look at your purchase and search history, then suggest similar content you might enjoy. When coupled with user generated reviews, which is a step above word-of-mouth marketing and one of the most effective forms of online advertising, you'll get the most bespoke automated suggestions for you.

Fun Fact:

In the first quarter of 2012 when Amazon introduced its "suggestion engine" the sites sales went up 29% because it made it easier for people who were searching within their niche interest to find more products and content to purchase [2].

People buy from people, and a recommendation engine is simply taking people's recommendations and automating them. This works for free content as well as paid - because not all of your friends are awake at 3am to tell you which YouTube videos you might like to watch.

By making it easy to discover new content in "niche" areas you take the mass market of people (green section above) who previously would only purchase from the limited selection in high street stores and push them along the Long Tail (orange section above) and allow them to buy from individual artists.

These services are not just limited to online stores. YouTube and newspapers do a similar job of recommending content based on your history to help you discover more niche content which the mainstream overlooked.

Advantages of the Long Tail include –

- Consumers can follow recommendations and explore new artists and content easier than ever before.
- It creates a larger, more diverse entertainment marketplace as the playing field is level online. An artist can self publish a book, film or TV show at a lower cost and people can discover it at a time and in a format which suits them.
- It treats people as individuals with varied interests. No longer are we seen as a generic group of people who all want the same thing. We're treated as a unique person and given the freedom to explore our interests as much or as little as we like.
- It allows artists to find an audience for what they do easier than ever before.

Disadvantages of the Long Tail include –

- A low barrier to entry means no quality control. The very fact that it's easy and free for anyone to upload anything means the quality can vary massively from one person's upload to another.
- Some content creators will get overlooked and struggle to make a living. In a crowded, abundant marketplace there's only a limited number of people who can succeed. If you find yourself in an area where too many other people are doing something similar to you, you'll have to change, become more unique or create a stronger connection with your core fans.
- Downward pressure on prices. Where there's abundance of something the thing is worth less (which is why we develop a relationship with our audience so we can sell to them on an emotional and personal level).

To sum up…

- You should aim for a niche pocket of people who aren't being catered to and so they are hungry for content.
- The Long Tail Theory is an economic model that shows how the "market" (aka everyone in the world's attention) has shifted away from focusing on mainstream products at the head of the demand curve towards a massive, ever widening number of niches at the tail.
- Half of all books sold on Amazon aren't available in shops. They're self published works sold directly from the writer to the readers.

CHAPTER 6
How many Fans do you really need?

The short answer is around 1,000.

The long answer is much more interesting.

In 2008 the founding executive editor of Wired magazine, Kevin Kelly, came up with the 1,000 True Fans theory [1].

To understand his theory we need to define a "True Fan" (or "Super Fan"):

In his own words: "A True Fan is defined as someone who will purchase anything and everything you produce. They will drive 200 miles to see you sing. They will buy the super deluxe re-issued hi-res box set of your stuff even though they have the low-res version. They have a Google Alert set for your name. They bookmark the eBay page where your out-of-print editions show up. They come to your opening shows. They have your signed copies. They buy the t-shirt, and the mug, and the hat. They can't wait till you issue your next work. They are true fans."

1,000 Fans doesn't sound like many, but if we look at the figures you'll see 1,000 True Fans (and in some cases fewer) are enough to make a good living and continue creating things you love.

The key to creating a True Fan is <u>communication</u>.

In all good relationships two-way communication between the people involved is the most important thing. Before the Internet this happened when magazines would interview artists so Fans would know more about them. Now we have social media sites that allow a real-time personal contact between creators and Fans.

To make themselves more money social media sites like Facebook and Twitter have made it feel like a competition. By publicly showing your "fans" or "follower" count it's easy to be sucked into the game of online Freeloader Fan acquisition. Your job is to avoid seeing social media as a competition and focus on building your audience of True Fans, after all they're the ones who are most likely to financially support you.

That's not to say the Freeloader Fans have no value. They provide a social context in which your paying Fans will get more out of funding your art. Even if 100,000 people who know your work wouldn't buy what you do, the fact the 1 person who did buy your painting can name drop means they get the prestige and pride of owning it.

Case Study.
In early 2015 comedian Richard Herring wanted to make another series of his podcast "Richard Herring's Leicester Square Theatre Podcast" (RHLSTP). Lacking funds he turned to his audience and created a crowdfunding campaign on KickStarter.com [2]

He set his target at £30,000. It took 1,156 backers to get get this target (and more - £33,146).

Richard had created 6 seasons of his show before asking the audience for a penny. Thus proving he cannot only deliver high quality content on a consistent basis but he'd created a relationship with his audience through in-jokes and recurring punchlines.

Beyond the podcast his work has gone up as well:

> *"Within a year or two of starting podcasts my live audiences had doubled (from admittedly quite a small number), but it certainly helped to make touring a viable way of making a living. Made new fans, reminded old ones I existed. Lots of people would say they listened to the podcast after."*
>
> *- Richard Herring*

So although he was only breaking even on his free content it was leading to paid work in other areas of his career. And all it took was 1,156 True Fans to sponsor him online to keep his content free.

In Kevin Kelly's theory a True Fan spends an average of $100 a year on you. That's $100,000 per year, which is a good wage by anybody's standards.

Most importantly of all this is achievable, as Kevin puts it: "One thousand is a feasible number. If you added one fan a day, it would take only three years. True Fanship is doable. Pleasing a True Fan is pleasurable, and invigorating. It rewards the artist to remain true, to focus on the unique aspects of their work, the qualities that True Fans appreciate."

> *These people are supporting you and show interest in you. So they become more invested in you as a unique product. This feeling and connection helps keep a person a True Fan.*
>
> *An artist's job is to keep building their base of True Fans, while keeping old ones as well as creating fun high-quality content that keeps everyone happy and interested.*

A dedicated artist can find a home below the mainstream and far enough up the long tail (we'll cover this in the next chapter) and all it takes is approximately **1,000 True Fans**. This number will vary depending on what you make and how much it sells for but it gives you a really good insight into how few Fans you need to be profitable.

In reality Super Fans will often spend a lot more than $100 (or £100 depending on your country… I am only using the dollar sign as Kevin is American) a year if you give them a method to do so.

In order to find your True Fans you need to find your niche. For an artist that's whatever you do. Do what you love and do it well, then share it with the world and an audience will follow. The size of that audience might be small, but there's an audience for everything.

The 1,000 True Fans Theory is often criticized for not taking into account the high production costs for creators, but with technology and equipment prices dropping all the time and so many free platforms to share your content these seem unfounded. If they ever were true, they're not any more.

In the 6 years that have passed since it was first published on Kevin's blog the idea of creating a connection with a committed niche of diehard Fans is truer (and easier) than ever.

Case Study.

Comedian Luisa Omielan did her debut comedy hour in 2012 to great success. Two years later she did her follow up show and then decided she wanted to release this show on DVD. In her own words, "In the UK it takes time, money and high profile to get a recording like this and mamma's impatient". So she turned to her fans [3].

She had no TV exposure, no radio plays, and was not a household name. What she did have was a video that was going viral (and has since been played over 20 million times). This lead to a spike in people joining her social media profiles.

Although her fan base went up, these were freeloaders and casual fans. Her core audience are the ones who backed her crowdfunding campaign to get her DVD recorded.

She set her target at £10,000 and ended the month-long campaign with £11,057GBP raised by 353 people. These people included 4 super fans who gave her £1000 towards the filming of her show in exchange for a private performance for them and their friends.

It is unlikely any of those 4 people saw her viral clip and thought "I'll give this woman £1,000". It is more likely that those 4 people had seen her live and jumped at the chance to book her. This level of relationship doesn't happen overnight. It would have taken Luisa years to build such a strong bond and trust with these 4 fans that they believe she will do a great private show for them and their friends.

At the time of writing this Luisa has 90,000 Facebook fans and 8,500 twitter followers. Not allowing for crossover that's nearly 100,000 fans... but she only needed 353 to reach her goal. 0.36% of her audience was all it took to get £10,000 to fund her DVD recording.

If you estimate that a further 1,000 people in her audience didn't donate but helped her get exposure and shared her campaign with friends / family / relatives, it still only took her a total of 1,353 people (1.37% of her total audience) to help her reach her goal.

In order to further understand why you don't need a million fans to be a profitable artist you need to know the 80:20 principle.

The 80:20 principle states that 80% of the effects come from 20% of the causes.

Italian engineer, sociologist and economist Vilfredo Pareto generated the theory after observing that 20% of the pea pods in his garden contained 80% of the peas. It has since been proven to work in business and not just gardens.

In "Living Life the 80/20 Way" by Richard Koch [4] he says the distribution is claimed to appear in several different aspects relevant to entrepreneurs, business managers and freelancer artists. For example:

- **80%** of a company's profits come from **20%** of its customers
- **80%** of a company's complaints come from **20%** of its customers
- **80%** of a company's sales come from **20%** of its products

As we'll see later in the book **80%** of the funding for projects tends to come from **20%** (or less) of the fans.

We'll also see how **80%** (or more) of gigs for a band / performer / artist come from **20%** (or less) of promoters.

It is important for artists to realise that most of their audience will never pay money directly for what they do.

Artists are able to sell individual items, short runs or digital versions of their work at varying price points to a small section of their audience directly.

A modern digital artist often doesn't even need 20% of their audience to pay for what they do to remain profitable. The minority group of Super Fans will value your work so highly they will pay hundreds of times the amount a Casual Fan will which helps counteract the majority of your audience who will Freeload what you do.

It is now possible to create a large audience around a niche offering and give it away for free online. You give your work away for free online to become more discoverable.

To understand how the Internet has made it easier for freelancers and artists to be discovered we need to look at the rise of online selling, recommendation engines and the Long Tail Theory.

To sum up…

- The key to creating a True Fan is <u>communication</u>.
- To make themselves more money social media sites like Facebook and Twitter have made it feel like a competition. By publicly showing your "fans" or "follower" count it's easy to be sucked into the game of online Freeloader Fan acquisition. Your job is to avoid seeing social media as a competition and focus on building your audience of True Fans, after all they're the ones who are most likely to financially support you.
- A dedicated artist can find a home below the mainstream and far enough up the long tail and all it takes is approximately **1,000 True Fans**.
- The 80:20 principle states that 80% of the effects come from 20% of the causes.
- As we'll see later in the book **80%** of the funding for projects tends to come from **20%** (or less) of the fans.
- We'll also see how **80%** (or more) of gigs for a band / performer / artist come from **20%** (or less) of promoters.

CHAPTER 7
How can you be unique in your field?

The Internet has created an abundance of content. Because of this abundance of content, quality is the new currency. People no longer owe you their attention. If they're bored of what you're doing they can switch off or go do something else. To keep their attention you need to create consistent, unique, interesting and quality content.

The problem people have is the amount of options for things to do, watch, hear and see has gone up while we've still only got 24 hours in a day. With so much content and so little time the obvious solution is to ignore anything ordinary or commonplace.

How do you stand out? You become a Purple Cow.

When you see a cow for the first time it's new, exciting and different. Once you've seen 10 more cows they become boring, commonplace and unremarkable. Now if you see a Purple Cow in a field it becomes exciting again. It becomes something different you want to talk about.

In Seth Godin's 2005 book "Purple Cows" [1] he explains the difference between a company who is visible and who is not is defined by how remarkable what you do is. He says "The old checklist of P's used by marketers - Pricing, Promotion, Publicity - aren't working anymore. The golden age of advertising is over. It's time to add a new P - the Purple Cow."

The same is more true for performers and artists.
If you have nothing remarkable to talk about how can your fans spread the word about what you do?

Before the Internet, TV channels and other mass media made it very easy to spread ideas if you could afford it. Audiences would be almost forced to sit through adverts in order to watch the program they want to enjoy. Seth calls this "The TV-Industrial Complex". This is where you buy adverts during TV programs to get more distribution. You then use the distribution to sell more products and then use the profit from that to buy more ads. And then repeat the process indefinitely.

Some marketeers put "as seen on TV" on products. Consumers know that the only time this happens the brand has paid for the product to be shown on television but even though we know it, it feels like a selling point.

TV hasn't been a badge of legitimacy and assurance for quite some time.

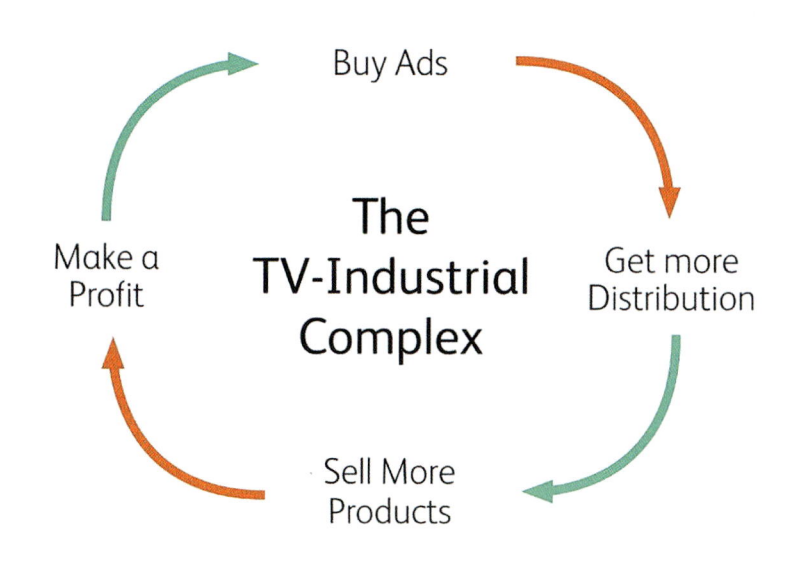

The TV-Industrial Complex

- Buy Ads
- Get more Distribution
- Sell More Products
- Make a Profit

There are two types of marketing you should be aware of [2]:

Interrupt Marketing

TV, radio, newspaper, pre-roll videos on YouTube clips and email spam adverts are examples of **interrupt marketing**. They get in the way of you watching or enjoying something to tell you about a product you might not be interested in. It's considered an annoying way of increasing awareness of a product, company or artist.

It has the advantage of getting the message of a product or service in front of a large group of people but the disadvantage that a lot of those people will not be interested in the message.

Permission Marketing

Permission marketing is where you have obtained permission from the person before advertising to them. Examples of this include asking people to "opt-in" to an email newsletter or getting them to follow you on Twitter.

It's largely used online and has the advantage that your message only goes to the people who want to hear it but has the disadvantage of going out to a smaller group of people. However this smaller more niche group of people are cheaper to contact and have a higher likelihood of buying something from you or sharing the message you want to spread.

As an artist, you want to focus on **permission marketing**. You want a dedicated group of people who are interested in what you do and have to say.

In 2011 comedian Louis CK released his stand up special as a download on his website. He marketed it through his mailing list which he had been growing for a number of years. He said "I made the web designer include a big button so nobody could miss it that said 'click this if you want me to email you in the future when I have stuff you can buy'". And it worked.

He has a massive mailing list (although the exact number is a closely guarded secret) which helped him generate one million dollars gross revenue in the first 12 days after releasing his 2013 DVD special. That means he sold 200,000 digital downloads directly to his fans.

His 2013 tour of the US, Canada and the UK sold out and was only sold through his website and marketed directly using his mailing list and Twitter. He has gone on record saying that this method has kept costs low which meant he could charge less for tickets, leading to more people being able to afford to see him live.

It's worth noting that in the United Kingdom, an opt-in has been required for email marketing, under The Privacy and Electronic Communications (EC Directive) Regulations 2003 since 11 December 2003 [3].

The question is: how do you build a base of people who care about what you do with so much content online?

The Internet has your potential fan's attention spread across multiple platforms and they can pick and choose the messages they want to see (**permission marketing**), as a result the TV-industrial complex doesn't work the way it used to (**interrupt marketing**).

People online will keep looking for the messages from artists and creators whose work they value and feel a connection with. They pass on messages or content that is remarkable and don't like being advertised to.

> "The thing that decides what gets talked about, what gets done, what gets changed, what gets purchased, what gets built is: is it remarkable? And remarkable is a really cool word. Because we think it just means 'neat' but it also means 'worth making a remark about.'"
> – SETH GODIN

Once you've picked a platform / social media site you want to showcase your work on always ask before uploading: "how will my audience be able to talk about this to their friends?". If you can't think of a way that they can tell someone else about it you might want to rethink the platform you are using.

Please note, not everything you put online has to be remarkable. Sometimes it's nice to wish your audience a "Merry Christmas" or thank them for sharing your content. But the advice above is for your best work which should be an idea that you want to spread.

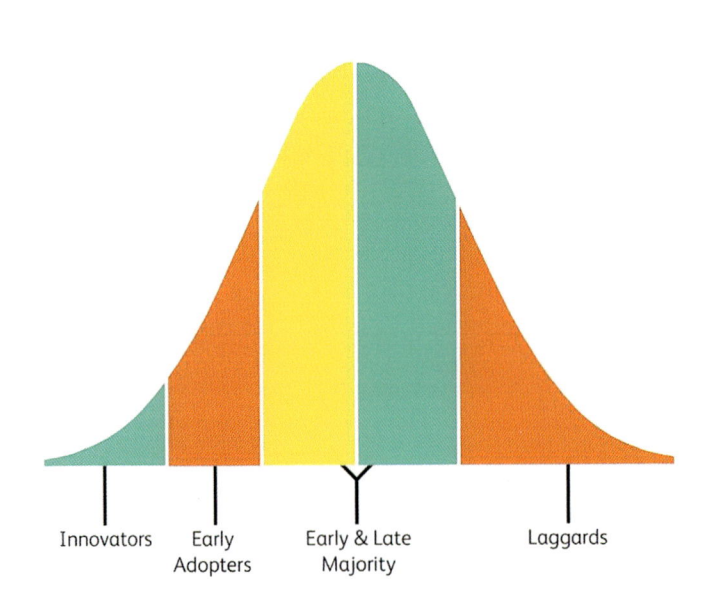

Innovators | Early Adopters | Early & Late Majority | Laggards

Before the Internet the vast majority of marketing professionals aimed their messages at the mass market (the yellow / green peak above). Today this doesn't work as well because these people are *really* good at ignoring adverts.

They've seen it all before and it takes a lot of time and effort to reach them and the cost has gone up massively.

However by targeting the Innovators (green) or Early Adopters (orange) you can get a niche group of diehard Fans interested. This leads to positive word-of-mouth **marketing at the mass market** (yellow / green peak above) easier, cheaper and more organically than ever before.

YouTube musician Smooth McGroove is an a cappella singer who covers 1990s video game soundtracks. He has over 1 million subscribers on YouTube. A million people love his content and want to watch his next music video. A "niche interest" doesn't always mean a small number [4].

He releases an album of covers every year which sell well but he has a diehard base of 789 fans who are patrons of his work and give him $2,579.19 per video (at the time of publishing). He uploads 2-3 videos per month. Which means without CD sales (or the pocket change that is ad revenue) he earns between $5,000 and $7,700 per month just from free videos. And at any time more of his audience can join his other patrons and help him earn more for all his hard work.

Word-of-mouth marketing

Word-of-mouth marketing is the most valuable form of advertising. We're all more likely to watch, listen or try something that has a personal recommendation from someone we trust the opinion of. This is nothing new. Advertisers have paid celebrities to endorse products for years but now we value our friends and family circles more when discovering art and content.

When you talk to the Innovators (green) or Early Adopters (orange) they listen because they **like listening to messages**. They enjoy being first and having the social status of knowing about something before everyone else. They won't all be interested in what you do, but they'll be the type of person who will pass it on to someone who is.

Otaku is a Japanese term for people with obsessive interests. We all have a friend who has Otaku. These people say "have you seen this video on YouTube?" or "you've got to try a sandwich from the restaurant that just opened up". They can't help it; they love to obsess over the latest and most interesting things and more importantly love to share it.

Talk to people who are listening and they'll tell their friends. The easiest way of talking to people is to give them something for free to hear what you have to say at a very low risk to them. The free digital content is easily shareable and will be passed around by being with Otaku to their friends.

Comedian Stewart Lee has taken the concept of picking one platform to build an audience to the extreme. He only has an email mailing list which you can only join via his website. He refuses to join Facebook, Twitter or any other social network. In fact he's done jokes about how useless the platforms are and anyone on them is impersonating him.

As a result if you want to find him you have to seek him out. Which suits his "outsider" style of comedy. He used to belong to one of the biggest comedy management companies but left them stating "they saw comedy as the new rock and roll so put us up in really expensive hotels which meant even if you sold out a tour you weren't left with much money to live off".

He built his own audience and mailing list and sold tickets direct to his fans. He drove to gigs and stayed in cheap BnBs. "I figured out if you can get 2,000 people to give you £10 or so per year that's a good wage. And you can build off that."

The internet has enabled artists to cut costs on everything except the show making your bottom line lower meaning you end up with more profit to live off. Think about how you can save money and you'll need to earn less to end up with the same amount in your bank.

As an artist the way you stand out and become remarkable is by giving away unique and exciting content for free. Safe is boring and in a world of niche interest boring gets discarded and ignored fast.

The riskiest thing you can do as an artist is play it safe.

Think of an artist whose work you enjoy. What makes them different or unique? What do you say about their work to friends? What is the "pitch" to your friends you say when they come up in conversation? Now ask the same questions of your work. Be honest… are you remarkable? What would make someone think of you if they needed to book someone?

On the comedy circuit a lot of acts try and play it safe and not offend anyone as they believe that's the easiest way to become a sellable act. But in reality you're harder to sell as there's hundreds of you because you blend in.

There are millions of artists and illustrators but what makes you unique is the way you draw. Don't try and blend in and be the best sketch artist by the book. Aim higher and develop your own style.

This works to a certain extent in acting as well. Yes there are more roles for pretty blonde haired women and muscular dark haired men but those are the roles everyone is trying to fill. If you looked different and memorable people will come running when they need an extra with dreadlocks or a lead character with a purple handlebar moustache.

This sounds hard to do but even if the thing you create is being done by thousands of other people you can make it unique by putting your own spin on it. There are hundreds of makeup tutorials on YouTube, but can you find a niche doing extreme zombie makeup? Or taking "looks" from music videos and showing how they can be done?

Key Point -

For your work to be spreadable it needs to have a simple sentence-long pitch that your fans can use to tell their friends, families and loved ones. This can be as easy as "he does Britney Spears covers on a ukulele" to "they do Monty Python sketches in Chinese". This sentence is key to gaining the interest of someone who currently doesn't know anything about your work… if this isn't easy for the fan to formulate they're not going to be able to spread the word of your work.

You can provide them a sentence of what you do as a pitch in your "about me" section on social media profiles or even at the start of every episode / video if appropriate. Several YouTubers start videos with variations on the format "hello, and welcome to the video series where I juggle fire in different locations". Rewording that into a pitch is easy for a fan to do: "he juggles fire in weird locations and records people's reactions".

Think about your audience, but don't let it impact the creative nature of the art itself.

People are shown so many messages in a day it's important to make yours stand out for it to be memorable. Former US Memory Champion Joshua Foer explains the best way of making something memorable is by making it stand out in your mind, then all associated information will be clearer as well. For example, if I asked you what you had for lunch yesterday you might remember. If I asked what you had for lunch the day before you might need a little more time but might remember it. If I asked you what you had for lunch 3 weeks ago you would need clues and prompts to make the memory clear in your mind if you could remember it at all. This is because all of your lunches have been grouped together in your memory as "lunch". The day you went to a fancy restaurant instead of a sandwich bar or met a schoolfriend you hadn't seen for ten years rather than the person who works across the office to you as you usually do will stand out more because it's different and noteworthy. The same theory works with artists: make something unique and interesting and it'll stand out to the audience that enjoyed it. Then your name and other information will be easier to remember because it's associated with the interesting thing they enjoyed [5].

Being memorable is simply the art of being unique.

In terms of making memories we can all think of a funny YouTube clip or a mindblowing TED talk or an interesting podcast or even a TV episode we re- ally enjoyed. This is because the content of that specific show resonated with us. It caused our minds to work hard to make a new section of our memory to store the content in because it didn't fit any of the pre-existing categories in your brain. Anything that people can ignore or file away as "just another musician / filmmaker / comedian" makes you forgettable and dull. **Be daring and stand out.**

Love or hate her Katie Hopkins is masterful at standing out. She's unapologetic about her views and as a result has a diehard loyal fan base of people who believe the same thing as her.

Controversial performer Dapper Laughs is the same. His online content either turns on or off people because of the attitude and strong angle he takes on everything.

Even if you hate one of the two names above, you remember them.

By being yourself and doing what you want people have something to talk about - for better or worse.

Aim to make "niche content" because then you're the one who connected with them in a new way that nobody else has done. This is how you create a deep meaningful relationship with an individual creating Super Fans. Super Fans are the first to give you the most valuable form of advertising: word-of-mouth.

If you believe in your artwork, statistically somcone else will enjoy it and because you're no longer geographically limited to where you can distribute your art, the world is your oyster. It doesn't guarantee it will be immediately profitable or sustainable but it does increase your chances of being interesting enough to be remarkable. And being remarkable is the key to building an audience.

Something being interesting and remarkable is the reason we share things. It's why a good, solid, consistent and quality performer is more likely to have their video shared. It's why you as an artist cannot afford to play it safe online.

Be honest with yourself before you click "upload" and ask these questions:

- Would you share this content?
- Would you recommend it to a friend?
- What would you say to a friend when sharing it?
- Will you remember this content in a month's time?

Why do you have to give stuff away?

So you've made something great and you're ready to share it with the world for free (or at a low cost), but you still fear the pirates.

You'll never completely get rid of the piracy of your work if it's good – even if you give it away for free. There will always be one person who feels the need to share it again somewhere. Once you accept this fact of life, you can move forward and try to reduce the number of reasons people will feel they have to pirate your work. To understand this, you'll need to know the main reasons why a person might pirate someone's art. These include -

1. To share information / content with someone else.

If your content is not readily available to a section of the world or is restricted to one group of people your fans will help others enjoy your work. This isn't necessarily a bad thing, but the lack of availability is. The only exception to this is limited editions where the reason for the restricted numbers is to add value and scarcity to the product. But if it is available in the UK and fans in the US have to wait a week, they'll pirate.

Another big reason for this piracy is because people want to introduce someone to your work. Before the internet people would lend CDs or DVDs for people to watch and enjoy. If they liked it enough, they would go out and buy a copy for themselves.

One of the biggest misconceptions online is that a "view" or "play" means the person enjoyed it. On YouTube the view count goes up regardless of how much (or little) you enjoyed the clip. On every social media platform you'll need to overlook the vanity metrics and focus on the ones that build your community.

Example
This often happens for newspapers who put up paywalls. Online information freedom is a big deal and by hiding information from the public you're just asking for someone to take it and republish it somewhere else.

In the first 4 month of having an online paywall The Times lost 90% of its readership. You could look at that and say they lost a lot of sales, or you could look at that and say they lost a lot of potential longterm relationships. Forgetting about the lost corebase of readers The Times has stopped anyone who wants to discover its content and maybe switch from another paper.

The readers didn't want to pay for the content at the amount they wanted to charge. A much better way of doing this would have been to allow readers to give what they think it's worth. This means the Super Fans of the publication would be able to give more than the £1 subscription price if they felt they were getting value from the paper.

A much better investment for The Times would have been to encourage community and conversation within the comments section of articles. This would have given them a unique selling point to any other newspaper as you can read the news and then have "watercooler talk" online directly after learning what's happened. They could reward users for taking part in discussions with levels of contribution and really built an area online where people would go to learn the news and beyond [6]

> Solution - When you publish some work, make it available globally at the same time unless there's a very good reason why you can't.

2. To gain credit on a file sharing website

Many private file-sharing sites offer a points system for every upload you do to the site. You can only download the same number of things you share on the site. This encourages people to upload and stay active on their network. However it does also encourage people to share content that might be available elsewhere for free.

> **Potential Solution - Ask your fans not to share your work. And if they do, to credit you. This will stop a small percentage who want to help you, but ultimately you need to look at this as someone unintentionally helping you reach more people.**

3. To pass it off as their own work.

This happens more often than you would think and is a horrible, sad fact. A lot of unimaginative or uncreative people will try and pass off the work of someone else as their own. With the rise of brands on social media and the cost of getting creative going up, some brands and people have taken to stealing other people's content and passing it off as their own.

> **This is clearly wrong and shouldn't happen.**

> **Potential Solution - Include date and time stamps on your uploads which makes it easier to prove it's your work. But as these can sometimes be edited, it's very hard to solve.**

4. They believe the price is unjustified or too expensive.

If the cost of legally buying the content they want is too high people will get it for free. One of the biggest changes online in the last few years is that it has become cost-effective for people to pay-what-they-like for art. This allows a basic digital download version of your art to go for as little as 1p but as much as the person can afford. This is The Curve (**Chapter 3: Where are you at the moment?**) in practice. What you think your work is worth might be completely different to everyone else who wants to buy it. Paradoxically, just because you're good at something (drawing, playing the piano etc) you might value that skill less than someone who admires someone who creates that thing.

This is why you give them a sample. So they can find the value in your work to validate the price you've put it for sale at. Trying your work for free is the most entry-level way of getting someone to think about paying for what you do, creating an emotional bond with them makes them want to support you financially with less thought or concern.

> **Potential Solution - Offer the product for free (or at a really low cost) for people to sample. If you're a musician this could be uploading it to Spotify, if you're a comedian it could be uploading a video to YouTube.**

5. Someone has purchased the art legally in another format but now wants it on their new device.

Because of the number of devices available this is happening more and more. Someone downloads an app on their iPhone, then they upgrade and get an Android phone and that person has to pay to get that app on their new device. How annoying!

> **Solution - Offer customers the option of getting their purchase in an alternative format for free (or at a discount rate). Also, make sure you have a way people can contact you directly to ask questions and explain their situation.**

6. "I'm only hurting a big business" syndrome.

Some pirates believe that illegally sharing art is only damaging "big businesses" so what's the harm? They've the money to absorb the cost. "Musicians don't see the money from album sales anyway, that all goes to the label" is something

I've heard far too often. Although this can be true, you need to make it clear if it isn't.

By selling direct to your fans you can minimise this reasoning even if you're with a major distributor. By having an honest and open relationship with your fans you can explain that your film / CD / download is being re-released through a major label and why you've chosen to do that.

Please note this is very different to when a major label buys your film script and makes it themselves. When this happens the public then has to decide if the film is worth the money based on a whole host of factors.

Solution - Have a one-on-one relationship with your audience where you're open and honest about what you did to make it so they know they're not ripping off a business, they're hurting an independent artist.

By knowing the reasons behind why people pirate art online you can reduce the chances of people illegally sharing your work by:

1. Creating great art.
2. Making it easy to buy.
3. Releasing it the same day worldwide.
4. Making sure it works on any device.
5. Selling it for a fair price (or let your audience pay what they want).
6. Having transparency about how the payments affect your ability to create more art (or not).

By doing all these things you reduce the number of people who will want to pirate your work and increase the number of people who will want to legally purchase it from you.

Reason why people will pay for free content.

By this stage of the book you should be convinced free high-quality content will help you build an audience that you can sell your work to in the future.

Even with all this theory I am often asked if in practice will people put their hands in their pocket and pay for something they can get for free.

The short answer is yes, but this is rarely enough to convince anyone. Most people want facts, reasons and statistics to back up a bold statement like that. If you are the type of person who would never pay for free content to support an artist, this book was probably not for you. You're the hardest person to convince of this fact because you're a Forever Freeloader. And that's fine, but I believe this group is an ever-narrowing subculture of people who believe they can have everything for free and never support the creator.

Hopefully this book has made you think about that PayPal account with a few tens of pounds in it, and you're starting to get itchy fingers over that podcast series you've been enjoying every morning on the way to work. Maybe your days as a Freeloader are numbered? If so, check out http://simoncaine.co.uk/

Below are several reasons why a person might choose to pay for something they could otherwise get for free. See how many apply to you and an artist you've supported the work of recently:

- **To support the artist they value.**
- Most people are aware that doing anything artistic for a living is hard work with no guaranteed payment in the end. People who do not create things often over estimate the cost and time something took to be made. As a result in order to help an artist continue making the things they value they're willing to pay.

    KickStarter and PayPal have enabled artists to ask their fans to pre-order merchandise or support them making more content. As a creative person you often forget how hard it is for someone else to make the things you create and how much they value that you did.

- **To make a statement.**
- Some artists go the independent route because they're seen as too "niche" or a "big risk" by the mainstream media / publishing industry.

By supporting someone who was seen as a "risk" they're sending a message to the industry as a whole that the artist in question is worth backing but also that the type of work they make is worth publishing.

Spoken word poet Shane Koyczan released his third book through KickStarter as "publishers didn't seem interested in books of poetry. The shelf space for it (poetry) in shops is getting smaller and smaller". He urged his fans to buy a physical copy of the book so they could show the publishing industry there's still a market for books. In 30 days he sold 632 physical books and 144 digital copies.

- **They're used to paying / historical legacy.**
- People of a certain generation have only known the system where they go to a shop and buy something created by an artist they enjoyed for free on the radio or TV. Old habits die hard and as a result this section of the market will continue to buy merchandise as a means to support the artists whose work they value.

The "silver surfer" generation online is growing by the day (these are people over the age of 50 who now have access to the internet). These people are used to paying for things they value and also have a bigger disposable income so often donate more than the average to help an artist out. They also have more life experience and so know how hard it is to make a living normally, let alone a way which isn't guaranteed, like being an artist.

- **Convenience of a different medium.**
- It's great watching a YouTube tutorial showing you how to make an origami swan, but what if you cannot try out the technique at your desk due to lack of space? Or if you want to see the technique written down to get off the computer for an hour? You might need to buy a book in order to read the instructions in a more convenient place.

Tim Ferriss released a digital copy of his third book "The 4-Hour Chef" through Bit Torrent. The book was about breaking down all the practical skills involved in cooking so that people can teach themselves how to do almost anything in a kitchen. Although a great resource the book isn't that easy to read digitally. The bundle (which contained most of the book along with case studies that didn't make it in as well as behind the scene content from the making of the book) was downloaded 2 million times. But the book still made it into the New York Times Best Sellers list. [9]

- **Limited Editions.**
- If you feel a deep connection with an artist it's often not enough to just own a CD or a print of a painting - you want more. You want the original painting or the deluxe CD with handwritten lyrics. These unique, sometimes one-off artefacts come at a high price even though these fans can often listen to the music on Spotify for free or browse the artwork on the artist's website for absolutely no money.

    Musician Julia Nunes ran a KickStarter in 2015 in which she offered backers the chance to buy a Ukulele case, but limited it to the first 30 backers. By making this run a limited number it made the value of them go up as the number available to buy was scarce. This meant she was able to charge $90 (or more) for a case and signed CD of her work.

- **Additional content.**
- Very often artists will give additional content away in paid products like early sketches, unedited scripts, background information on the art itself etc. They also offer content that they didn't want to share for free as it becomes more exclusive to those invested fans that purchased their work.

    Patreon.com has allowed dedicated fans of an artist to pledge to back them every time they bring out new content. By doing so, the artist has a budget for their art and a promised number of sales. In exchange for their dedication the artist can offer them exclusive perks for backing their on-going work or exclusive content which is only available to Patrons.

- **Gifts.**
- Having a product to purchase allows fans to share an artists work with someone they love. It helps spread the word of that artist to another person and gives them a much more bespoke gift.

    A prime example of this would be a YouTube cookery blog and buying their recipe book for a family member who doesn't use YouTube to find recipes. This links well to "convenience of a different medium" (see above).

    YouTube channel SORTED Food was started in March 2010 by a group of friends who were learning how to cook. It now has over 800 free video tutorials on YouTube. Although they have a regular base of viewers on that platform they will make more money from the sales of their physical and digital books than the adverts on the clips. They've proven time and time again that they can cook and know what they're doing, so their loyal audience of more than 1 million subscribers will buy from them. They won't all, but as long as 1000 do, they are sustainable.

- **Social status.**
- There's a social status to owning anything. By owning a book, CD or DVD by an artist you're making a statement about your tastes and interests. When friends come over they can browse your music collection and get an idea of what you like (and what you don't).

    Visual artist Linus Lee makes high quality explicit cards written in calligraphy fonts. To do the first run of the series he offered his early backers cards for less money than the normal rate as well as options to buy some of limited edition cards which you can only get through the IndieGoGo crowd funding campaign. This means you'll be sending your friend a card which is not only high quality but is also unique.

Remember: having 100,000 freeloader fans who know what you do helps increase the social status value of owning some of your work for your Super Fans. To a Super Fan, knowing that 100,000 people know what you do makes you famous, which means they have bragging rights and an artefact which is only going to go up in value as you work hard to move the Freeloader Fans to fanhood and then (for the select few) to Super Fan status. [7]

- **Knowledge / reference.**
- Sometimes it's nice to have an offline version of something you value. This could be for the fact you want a copy in case you cannot find it online at a future date, or because you want to have a reference / easy place to find the information should you not be able to get online for some reason.

  Also, if your computer is off and you want to cook something it's easier, faster and cheaper to open a book instead of turn on your computer and finding the recipe you're after - You're also in less danger of spilling egg on your keyboard!

- **The art might not be something you'd buy, but you would help pay for.**
- YouTube videos aren't something you'd want to purchase a copy of, but the creator might be someone you want to support and help continue creating. Patreon.com is an on-going crowdfunding platform which allows a creator's biggest fans the chance to offer to back their future content creation. We will discuss this platform in more detail later in the book.

  Video blogger Hannah Witton has been making videos since 2011. She has over 100,000 subscribers and rarely sells merchandise. She blogs about her life and the history of sex, sexual health and sex positive subjects. She started a Patreon page where people could sponsor her to help her continue making videos. 48 people now patronise her and donate $821 in total per video she uploads. The

> videos are available for free, but her Super Fans want to pay for her videos - something you can't buy [8].

How many artists make things that you love but that you wouldn't want to buy a copy of? That doesn't mean you wouldn't want to support them, it just means you don't want or need a copy.

This market is growing rapidly. And in a world of niche interests a lot of people have a message, sense of social responsibility or core value which informs their content. Everyone has a sense of right and wrong and if that informs some (or all) of your content you're more likely to attract a stronger bond with a potential audience member. Much like making a friend or picking a partner, you're more likely to feel a connection with someone who shares your values and ideals. But on the flip side it will also attract hate from people who have an opposing viewpoint.

- On Instagram and Flickr photographers are sharing their work for free. You might not want to buy a print but you might want to support them creating more content.
- On YouTube vloggers are sharing behind-the-scenes updates from tours and while you would not want to buy a copy of this, you might want to reimburse the creator for their time and effort.

Supporting something you do not want to buy makes sense as soon as you've found one creator who shares their work with you and you don't want a copy of it, but you do want them to create more.

To sum up…

- How do you stand out? You become a **Purple Cow**.
- TV hasn't been a badge of legitimacy and assurance for quite some time.
- There are two types of marketing you should be aware of: **Interrupt Marketing** & **Permission Marketing**.
- People online will keep looking for the messages from artists and creators whose work they value and feel a connection with. They pass on messages or content that is remarkable and don't like being advertised to.
- A "niche interest" doesn't always mean a small number.
- Word-of-mouth marketing is the most valuable form of advertising.
- *Otaku* is a Japanese term for people with obsessive interests. We all have a friend who has Otaku. These people say "have you seen this video on YouTube?" or "you've got to try a sandwich from the restaurant that just opened up". They can't help it; they love to obsess over the latest and most interesting things and more importantly love to share it.
- The internet has enabled artists to cut costs on everything except the show making your bottom line lower meaning you end up with more profit to live off.
- The riskiest thing you can do as an artist is play it safe.
- Think about your audience, but don't let it impact the creative nature of the art itself.
- Being memorable is simply the art of being unique.
- By being yourself and doing what you want people have something to talk about - for better or worse.
- Aim to make "niche content" because then you're the one who connected with them in a new way that nobody else has done.
- You'll never completely get rid of the piracy of your work if it's good – even if you give it away for free.
- Remember: having 100,000 freeloader fans who know what you do helps increase the social status value of owning some of your work for your Super Fans.

CHAPTER 8
Why advertising undervalues content.

People's information streams have become individually customisable. As a result traditional advertising is less effective because people can switch off or block permanently the messages they don't want to see in favour of the artists or niche content creators whose work they value.

The short answer is: Advertisers don't care how excited you are about the art. Creators do.

The long answer is much more interesting…

As artists your job is 50% creating, 50% finding a way to monetize it.

> If you want to make a thing once, you don't have to worry about the money. You can take some time off work and use your savings and maybe you'll make a financial return but if you want to be an artist you need to think about how you get paid for what you want to do.

In **2009** a musician could upload a clip to YouTube and because there was less of an abundance of content online, they were able to be discovered easier and make more digital sales from one-off viewers from iTunes.

In **2016** an artist using YouTube doesn't make enough money through advertising because the price of advertising online has dropped. They also make less on digital downloads because they've had to share their music for free on other platforms like Spotify to increase the chance they'll become discoverable to new audiences.

Example

On the 31st July 2006 the rock band OK GO released their music video for their single Here It Goes Again. The video consisted of them dancing on treadmills in a single continuous take. The video went viral and was viewed 56 million times before they took it down. It has since been reuploaded in 2009 and viewed nearly 25 million times.

The music video won the 2007 Grammy Award for Best Short Form Music Video and the 2006 YouTube awards for Most Creative Video. OK Go performed the dance routine live at the 2006 MTV Video Music Awards.

All this press coverage helped people discover the band and helped push them into a more mainstream audience.

In both 2006 and 2009 a video with 1 million or more views was not commonplace. If someone sent you a video link with over a million views on it you'd be more likely to watch it. A video with an abnormal amount of views will get more people to think it has good quality or interesting content because we presume it has been shared a lot by people who enjoyed it and viewed by the people have been sent the link.

In 2016 more people and content are online which means there's more videos that have 1 million or more views. They're commonplace and although impressive, they're nowhere near as impressive as they once were.

Due to the fall in price of online advertising the amount of money content creators get paid has decreased with it. As a result an artist hoping to make real sums of money from online adverts needs enough of them to make the tiny margins work. Put simply: online advertising only works at scale.

In 2012 **YouTube** was getting 4 billion views [1] on the videos it hosted per day. It didn't need to pay to create any of this content as people from all over the world were doing it for them for free. As a result they can make money by showing adverts around the videos because they have little-to-no content creation costs.

As an **artist**, it's near impossible to get paid a living wage from adverts.

Say you're thinking about making money from uploading videos to YouTube.

Traditional advertising (like pre-roll adverts shown before YouTube clips) exist on a flat-fee per X number of views which means we can crunch the numbers.

Say you uploaded a video that gets **1,000,000** views.

Advertisers pay at a set CPM rate. CPM stands for "cost per mille" or "cost per thousand views". At £2 CPM the revenue for that video is £1,000. That gets split 50/50 with YouTube so you get £500 in your pocket.

These numbers are based around YouTube monetizing every view, which they do not.

In reality YouTube monetizes approximately 1 in 4 views depending on the number of advertisers paying to be displayed and the time of the year.

So now you're getting only £125 for **1,000,000** views.

It's really important to remember these aren't "*views*" or "*hits*" they are **people**. In a world of mass marketing it's very easy to forget we're dealing with individuals. Individuals who will all value what they've viewed in different ways.

As an artist, a view is someone taking the time to experience my art and I appreciate you as an individual.

As an advertiser you're 1/1000th of a CPM and your attention is worth £0.005.

Back to OK GO.

The music video for Here It Goes Again has been viewed **81,000,000** times.

At £2 CPM (which is very high by the way) the potential revenue for that video is £162,000.

But that's if every play had an advert, which it doesn't so divided by 4 leaves £40,500.

Split that with YouTube and the band is left with £20,250.

Which sounds a lot, but that's over the space of 8 years. Which works out £2531.25 per year.

But there's 4 of them in the band (assuming there was nobody else involved in the making of the video, which there was, but for the sake of simplicity we'll assume the money is only getting split between the members of the band.

That means for a 3 minute long video which got 81 million views each band member gets £632.81p per year (under £2 per day).

The single peaked at #36 in the UK Singles Chart on 1st October 2006 clearly generating more money for the band than the adverts. But more importantly it enabled them to tour to a wider audience. Their free content wasn't about making money through advertising, it was about establishing themselves as something unique and interesting.

When planning on sharing content for free, you must assume you will not make money from it. It's about reaching people, not profit at this stage.

It's far better for an artist to create connections with an individual viewer and offer them the chance to give some money if they *valued* what they've just viewed or consumed.

Online marketers can be much more specific who sees their advert and bid on how much they'll be willing to spend. They can be as detailed as "all comedy videos from Michael McIntyre about his children" to as vague as "all how-to videos from the UK". As a result the amount of money an online content creator earns through adverts is low.

When content was scarce and we only had a handful of TV and radio channels to pick from the broadcasters used their monopolies to charge very high rates to advertisers. This is partly because it costs a lot to run and operate a TV channel but also they had the control over what people consumed. If you wanted to watch a soap opera you'd have to watch one of the limited ones that were available.

Online there's no monopoly over where people spend their time so advertising is worth a lot less. Paradoxically it's more targetable because people sign up to online accounts to consume content and give personal data like their age or gender or location or even their school. You can, if you want to, target your material directly at the Year 10 pupils of your old school and it won't cost you very much - if that's what you really want to do.

Think of any artists or content providers who you've discovered online. Sum up their work in one sentence how you might "pitch" them to a friend who has never seen them. Now try the same thing for what you want to create and share. That's your niche and where your value is at.

> **Do not chase short term financial gain at the expense of building long term sustainable relationships.**

To sum up…

- Advertisers don't care how excited you are about the art. Creators do.
- Put simply: online advertising only works at scale.
- It's really important to remember these aren't "*views*" or "*hits*" they are **people**. In a world of mass marketing it's very easy to forget we're dealing with individuals. Individuals who will all value what they've viewed in different ways.
- **As an artist**, a view is someone taking the time to experience my art and I appreciate you as an individual.
- **As an advertiser** you're 1/1000th of a CPM and your attention is worth £0.005.
- When planning on sharing content for free, you must assume you will not make money from it. It's about reaching people, not profit at this stage.

CHAPTER 9
How to think like a fan.

A great way of deciding what content you want to share or build is by asking yourself what you want to see made. If you cannot find it the way you think it should be done - do that.

Scratch your own itch first.

By deciding to do something for yourself you know there's at least 1 person in the target audience. From their you can share it and start to spread it.

This is in the very early stage of building a fanbase, you're looking for what makes you unique, interesting and remarkable.

A good starting point for this is forgetting your original aims you wrote at the start of the book and answering the following questions -

Here's my answers first...

As a **comedian** I really want to **see intelligent, dark comedy about subjects including race, gender, sexuality, feelings and relationships**.

Now I can go and make a list of artists whose work I admire and write a sentence (less than 25 words) describing their work the way I would pitch it to a friend in conversation who has never heard of them before -

1. **Stewart Lee** - He's a really intelligent stand up who does a lot of political material as well as cock jokes.
2. **Julia Nunes** - She's a musician who covers songs on YouTube. But she uses split screens to play all the instruments.
3. **Tim Ferriss** - He's a businessman / entrepreneur who writes books on how to effectively manage your time so you can focus on the things you want to do.
4. **Bec Hill** - She's a comedian who also does "paper puppetry" where she animates stick figures in real life to tell a story.

If you can't do this, you need to rethink what you're doing. It's no longer enough to just be funny or have a great singing voice - hundreds of people have that. You need something unique.

The sentence you use to describe yourself should fill the criteria of what you said you wanted in the first question. It doesn't need to cover all of it, but it should cover at least some of it.

When you have a sentence which describes you, your work has a direction and a word-of-mouth marketing hook. You can do much more than your "hook" but you have to have one.

> "in order to be famous you should have a look which people can recognise in silhouette"
> - RUSSELL BRAND

Although this book isn't about becoming famous, he still has a point. Very few bland, ordinary artists make a living because there's nothing for the audience to connect with.

10 years ago (before the internet really took off) I would read music magazines and see that my favourite musicians inspirations sometimes were the same bands I enjoyed. By feeling like we had something in common it gave me something to remember them by and connect with.

Your hook is your sales pitch which must be simple and identifiable to make word-of-mouth easier and more interesting to someone who doesn't know your work. Someone who doesn't know you, doesn't want to give you any time because they're busy. They'll give a friend 30 seconds to talk about you, but if they're not interested they'll switch off. This narrow gap of time is very important to remember when picking your "hook".

Now it's your turn. You don't have to show anyone these answers… ideally you won't need to, they'll work it out for themselves.

As a _____ I really want to see / make / create _____

_____.

Now go and make a list of artists whose work you admire and write one or two sentences (less than 25 words) describing their work the way you would pitch it to a friend in conversation who has never heard of them before -

See if you can get one from different artistic mediums (drawing / illustration, directing, writing, stand up, TV, radio, music etc)

1.

2.

3.

4.

Now it's your turn…

_____ - _____

[Your name above] - [Your one sentence desc]

Now you have a direction for your content and artwork we can look at what Fans (you) would want from what you're going to make.

The easiest way to understand what it is like to be a Fan is to remember that we're all a Fan of something. Even the most famous artist or creator has someone they look up to. Pick one of the 4 artists you listed above who closest matches your artistic medium.

Now quickly think of all the things that connect you with that artist. That make you feel like you know, like and respect them as creators.

Someone feels that for your work.

This is not a comfortable feeling because it's new to a lot of people. But by focusing on how you feel about your favorite creators you can understand the mindset of someone who loves what you do.

This is not only helpful when taking compliments or positive feedback for your work but it's also helpful when crowdfunding or trying to raise funds. On crowdfunding platforms you (the artist) are encouraged to give the backer (your fans) rewards for helping you out.

Thinking up rewards can be hard to do, but by remembering what you would want from someone whose work you adore you're able to think like a fan.

To sum up...

- Scratch your own itch first.
- By deciding to do something for yourself you know there's at least 1 person in the target audience. From there you can share it and start to spread it.
- When you have a sentence which describes you, your work has a direction and a word-of-mouth marketing hook.
- The easiest way to understand what it is like to be a Fan is to remember that we're all a Fan of something.

CHAPTER 10
Pick yourself.

The internet has given creative people the tools to make and share their creations at a very low cost. This is the best time in history for an independent artist to find their audience and be sustainable without mass appeal.

With all these tools at your disposal, pick yourself. Don't wait for an agent, PR company, management organisation or anyone to tell you that you can do this. You can do it with permission you give yourself. Make what you want to make, find a way of making it digitally available and share it with the world.

Before the internet if you were a sitcom writer you'd have to convince a channel to put your work out there. If you were a musician you'd have to get a label to sign you and fund your album. If you were a comedian you'd need an agent to open doors with people you weren't able to contact or even easily research the names of.

You can share your work and find an audience for it without asking for permission to put it somewhere online where the world can see it.

Think about that for a second... there are billions of people with access to the internet. And you can share your work online. You have a potentially larger audience than ever before, for a very low cost. So why wait for someone to pick you?

This isn't about treading water until that TV executive (or whoever) finds you and puts you on TV. The executive might give you £20,000 to write and star in a sitcom, which takes a year of your life to write and produce. A well-managed group of dedicated Super Fans may well pay you more than that and love your work more.

Waiting for an agent to pick you is foolish. It's a sign of insecurity and fear. You're waiting for them to come along so they're accountable if you're not successful. By allowing them to take some of the workload off your hands you can say "well, they didn't promote my CD enough". In which case why didn't you just do it better yourself? Even if they do it well... you have no idea how to replicate that should they decide to drop you.

"Industry" is an illusion of security. Because they look and sound like something secure. And in some ways they are... but much like every job with a boss you've ever had, they can fire you at any time. You're an artist because you want to work for yourself, so why would you pick to have a boss? I'm not saying shun the industry or turn down every bit of help you get (far from it). But pick people who support you and work with you or for you.

In the early stages of your career it's best to pick yourself because otherwise you'd never do anything. If you're always waiting for someone to discover how good you are at illustrating children's books you'll never put the time and effort in to learn the skills they'll need you to have if an agent rings you. By going it alone at the start you are in a much more powerful position further down the line should you want to work with others on your business. Because you'll know exactly what work they'll be taking off you and if it's something you need them to do. Think of it like being the intern at your own company starting at the bottom and learning all the jobs in the company before trying to employ someone to do that work.

Picking yourself is an empowering premise. It means you're able to do anything. And I mean anything. Want to make an album? Do it. You can put it on Spotify within minutes and share it with friends. This used to take weeks, months, maybe even years - before the internet levelled the playing field.

The only restrictions you have on what you can make are the time you have alive to make it and the equipment you need to make it the quality you want. The real question now is... what do you want to make? And how can you make it freely accessible for people to discover you?

To sum up...

- With all these tools at your disposal, pick yourself. Don't wait for an agent, PR company, management organisation or anyone to tell you that you can do this. You can do it with permission you give yourself. Make what you want to make, find a way of making it digitally available and share it with the world.
- Waiting for an agent to pick you is foolish. It's a sign of insecurity and fear. You're waiting for them to come along so they're accountable if you're not successful.
- "Industry" is an illusion of security.

CHAPTER 11
Why paywalls are the worst thing online.

Paywalls are an online system that stops people from accessing content on a website without a paid subscription. We know the biggest restriction of the subscription model is that it limits your biggest fans financial support but here are 4 more reasons why in the world of digital content they are a bad choice for an artist:

1) By hiding your content you're losing potential audience members and restricting new people from finding the work that you do.
2) You're pushing more casual fans away to other content providers where they can get the information for free. This means you're giving away potential fans to your competition who welcome them with open arms offering them things they can connect with.
3) Even if you have a base of paying customers at the moment you're not seeking out new audiences for when they stop deciding to pay. Paywall customers will only grow fewer over time unless you sink enormous resources into getting new ones.
4) You set the price you think your content is worth; this puts off a large amount of people who might pay less for it helping contribute to your revenue.

The music industry has had to adapt in recent years. They were hit hard in the 1990s with online piracy making music sales drop. They needed a new way of making money. Sadly, the music industry often asks the wrong questions like "How do we make people pay for music?" The real question should be "How do we allow people to pay what they want for the music they value?"

As we've seen everyone values what you do differently. In the case of online newspapers some people will only want to read a certain column they enjoy. Others will only want to read 3 or 4 articles on their football team. By charging them the same as someone who reads the whole newspaper you're making him or her feel like they're not getting value for money and you're not treating them as an individual. When newspapers only existed in physical formats it made sense to charge people for the full publication, as it wasn't cost effective to sell them individual sections or articles, online this is not only possible but also practical.

Ultimately putting up a paywall is like charging someone to browse your shop, and how many of us want to be charged just to look?

Offering online subscriptions to paywalls is even worse. It means you're setting a price you value your work at, which limits your biggest fans from supporting you as much as they'd like to. Subscription models have two variables: the number of free users and the number of paid users. The only way to make more money is to convert free users to pay the set price, but what if they don't value it the same as you do? What if they want to give you £1 instead of £2? You could be missing out on a large amount of revenue by sticking to a single price point as we've seen in the Curve.

I am the host of the Ask The Industry Podcast [1]. This podcast (at the time of writing) has 14 Patrons giving me a total of $51 per episode. 2 of my Patrons are donating $10 per episode. The average amount I'm being donated is $3.64. Clearly trying to calculate the value of my podcast using averages doesn't work.

My patrons break down like this —

Donation amount	Number of Patrons
$1	3
$2	6
$3	2
$5	1
$10	2

If I charged $3.64 for my podcast the 9 people donating less than that might not give me anything and anyone above that would be limited to less than they'd like.

Where possible you should allow people to pay what they value your work at.

My patrons love the show I produce and, although it is all freely available online, they want to support me and keep the show going.

Paywalls for artists are a bad idea in a world where there is so much competition and free content. A much more effective system is to ask your audience to become patrons of your work. A patron is someone who cares about what you do and wants to support it in exchange for gifts.

When Beethoven wrote his Fifth Symphony in 1804 he dedicated it to two of his biggest patrons by putting their names into the programme. This system is not new, it's just never been this easy and simple.

If you're an on-going content creator you're able to ask your audience to support you financially. It's now cost effective to show you're worth supporting through free content and regular communication with your audience and then tell them about your upcoming projects or need for on-going funding.

When you start making music, films or paintings you don't know if anyone is going to like or appreciate it you do it for the love of it or to experiment creatively. Once you've shared your work with the world and found some people who do, why wouldn't they want to help fund you to create more?

It means people can pay per piece of content you make which results in you wanting everything you create to be at the highest possible quality. The Internet has made it easy for fans to give however much they want for their work. It's an act of trust in the relationship between fan and artist for the creator to say "here is my work… enjoy it for free. But if you do enjoy it, please pay me to make more, because if nobody does, I can't." This act of trust helps build strong relationships between fans and artists.

A core bedrock of all relationships in life is communication and trust. Online you're able to be more transparent and honest with your audience. Trust in artists comes over time. It could be from first hand experiences with them and their work or a social proof of what they do. Either way this trust did not come overnight. And it shouldn't. People who trust too quickly are often disappointed because their expectations are too high. When trust comes over a few months or years it develops into realistic expectations and a connection built on real things.

Next we are going to see what metrics and numbers you should be focusing on as a community leader for your work.

To sum up…

- Sadly, the music industry often asks the wrong questions like "How do we make people pay for music?" The real question should be "How do we allow people to pay what they want for the music they value?"
- Ultimately putting up a paywall is like charging someone to browse your shop, and how many of us want to be charged just to look?
- When Beethoven wrote his Fifth Symphony in 1804 he dedicated it to two of his biggest patrons by putting their names into the programme. This system is not new, it's just never been this easy and simple.

CHAPTER 12
Vanity Figures.

It's easy in a world of social media to get swept away with vanity metrics and forget that's all they are. In some ways it's great to be able to see how many Followers, Fans and views friends and other creatives have, but it's important to keep them in perspective.

You are not your Follower count.

These numbers are reflective of a bigger view of your audience and the changing nature of developing relationships online. If you have a million views on a video on YouTube that doesn't mean it was amazing. There have been countless videos that got thousands of views because they were dreadful. You need to measure your success in other ways.

The only numbers you should be interested in are the ones which help you make decisions and get you to your goals. This could be releasing a CD or getting a live tour organised. Sadly most of the public data you get on social media sites are vanity figures, i.e. ones which are great to say, but don't actually tell you anything.

Equally, just because you have 100,000 followers on Twitter doesn't mean you're achieving your goal of being sustainable. 100,000 followers looks great on paper, but if they never come see you live and always freeload off your work you're going to go into debt quickly.

There are thousands of websites where you can buy Followers for your twitter account or Fans for your Facebook page but none of this matters if they don't have a connection with you and what you do. Buying people's attention takes you back to interrupt marketing and not permission marketing (which is where you want to be). For more info on this please see **"Chapter 7: How can you be unique in your field?"**

Old school marketing is based solely around numbers. The reason for this is because the only way to make more money is to sell more products. With the internet it is easy to offer all your fans the chance to support you at a price which suits them.

This doesn't mean that having a large Freeloader audience is a bad thing, but doing nothing to covert them into Fans is. By treating every Fan as the individual that they are you can focus on building a relationship with them that helps move them along The Curve. It also stops you trying to see your audience as one big group and instead focus on a much more useful and specific measure:

Revenue per individual fan

To calculate the revenue per fan we need to look at how you work out revenue in a non-digital way first.

Averages

In the world of digital sales the "average" can be very misleading.

In the mass market, where pricing is uniform, you can use the average to estimate sales as well as the amount an "average" person will contribute to your profitability. It doesn't work like that in a digital world.

Let's take a look at the numbers…

There are three types of average: the **mean**, the **mode** and the **median**.

The **mean** is the most commonly used average. It's where you add up all the different values in a set and divide them by the number of values involved. The mean is used to work out the common average among a set of numbers.

The **mode** is the value that appears most often in a set of data. This is used to work out what is the most popular item in a list of data.

The **median** is the middle value of a set of numbers. For example, if you had a list of people's shoe sizes: 1,3,6,10. The median would be 5.

In the book "The Black Swan" by Nassim Taleb he develops two imaginary countries, Mediocristan and Extremistan, to help explain his **Black Swan** Theory [1].

In short:

Mediocristan is where normal things happen, things that are expected, whose probabilities of occurring are easy to compute, and whose impact is not terribly huge.

Extremistan is where nothing can be predicted accurately and events that seemed unlikely or impossible occur frequently and have a huge impact. **Black Swan** events occur in Extremistan.

Nature has loads of examples of things that follow normal distribution, like people's height. If you saw ten people walking down the street, the odds are that most of them will be very close to the average height with maybe 1 or 2 being very short or tall. This is normal distribution (Mediocristan).

An example of something that doesn't follow normal distribution (Extremistan) would be a **Black Swan**.

Income distribution exists in Extremistan. Most people make close to the "average" salary. Some make less and a few make a massive amount.

Mean, mode or median are all properties of normal (or Gaussian) distribution and are a very simplistic way of viewing the world. This view only works in Mediocristan.

If you attempted to calculate the average UK salary using the **mean** using a select sample of 30 people the chances are that almost all the people in the group would make around the average. If you included everyone in the UK people like Richard Branson (whose net worth was £2.7 billion in 2013) will have a disproportionate impact on the "average".

One change had a disproportionate effect on the average.

Book sales, whether a movie becomes a hit, or viral YouTube clips all have similar characteristics, and therefore reside in Extremistan.

Extremistan is not governed by physical constraints.

Why is this relevant to you as an artist?

Any business or artist whose products can be made digital are moving from Mediocristan to Extremistan. This is because their audience or target group of consumers has increased massively. When you go from being an artist whose work is hard to discover to a musician on Spotify who has a large, global potential audience of fans who will all value your work differently you can see why the "average" becomes harder and harder to calculate.

When we see people as individuals we stop grouping them together and focusing on the "**average**" and focus on the **revenue per Fan**.

The more an individual Fan contributes to what you do the more time, effort and thanks you (the artist) give them in return.

How do you get measurable and non-vanity metrics?
ASK YOUR AUDIENCE.

By talking to your audience and asking them what they want you can get real-time responses and honest opinions which help you make better choices. If you want to record a CD and are thinking about crowdfunding, ask your audience if they'd be willing to back you. If you want to put on a tour and aren't sure where your biggest fans are, ask them if they'd like to see you live and if they do where they live!

Case and point...

Comedian Richard Herring has been touring with a new show every year for the last decade. By slowly building his fan base in small cities he's able to sell out bigger venues in counter-intuitive places. Why? Because he knows where his audience is.

How to find your fans location...

Almost every website or hosting service offers analytics. If you don't want to ask your audience where they are (and I would highly recommend that you do) you can always go into the backend analytics for your audience and see where they've listed themselves.

Below is a screenshot from my Twitter Analytics (you can find yours at http://analytics.twitter.com). Any user on Twitter can see their data for free. As you can see, I can get a rough estimation where my followers are located as a great starting off point to planning where I want to perform my show in the future.

Region

State or region	% of audience
England, GB	70%
Greater London, GB	32%
South East England, GB	9%
North West England, GB	6%
East England, GB	5%
South West England, GB	4%
Scotland, GB	4%
East Midlands, GB	4%
Yorkshire and The Humber, GB	4%
West Midlands, GB	3%

By having a dialogue with your audience and an on-going conversation with your biggest Fans you're able to see how close you are to your 1,000 True Fans and make great choices about the future of your career.

Never be afraid of asking your audience what they will and won't do for you. They've already signed up to get more information from you (if you've not purchased those likes / follows) so they're already interested in what you do, make or create.

Once you've worked out if you have some people interested in buying or funding your next project you need to know the best ways of financing it through the crowd you've created.

To sum up…

- You are not your Follower count.
- If you have a million views on a video on YouTube that doesn't mean it was amazing. There have been countless videos that got thousands of views because they were dreadful. You need to measure your success in other ways.
- The only numbers you should be interested in are the ones which help you make decisions and get you to your goals.
- Buying people's attention takes you back to interrupt marketing and not permission marketing (which is where you want to be).
- Old school marketing is based solely around numbers. The reason for this is because the only way to make more money was to sell more products.
- In the world of digital sales the "average" can be very misleading.
- Any business or artists whose products can be made digital are moving from Mediocristan to Extremistan.
- When we see people as individuals we stop grouping them together and focusing on the "**average**" and focus on the **revenue per Fan**.

CHAPTER 13
A Quick Guide to Crowdfunding.

Crowdfunding is a way of funding a project, venture or idea by raising money from a large group of people (backers). This works best over the internet as people from all over the world can discover your idea and fund it at a price which suits them.

Crowdfunding is the best way for artists to fund their work as it puts the power in the hands of their fans. This sounds scary, but if you've built up enough trust and respect within your audience they will want to help you to continue to make more of what you create.

In the book "The Art Of Asking" by Amanda Palmer [1] she emphasises the importance of her willingness to put her hand out and ask for support or help from her fans. When thinking about crowdfunding you should have the attitude to "trying it and seeing what happens". If you don't get your funding, you're not in a worse place than when you started. You're just more able to see where you are within your community and your relationship to those in it. Also, you can always ask again in 6 months when you have another 1,000 followers / subscribers / likes. It shows you still believe in the idea and want them to believe in it as well.

Only you know the "best time" to crowdfund your next project or existing content production. You're the person closest to your audience and so will get a feeling for when is good for them and you. It is worth coming up with the idea and forgetting costs to start with. Go crazy and decide what you want to do first. Once you've done that, then you can budget it out.

Don't go to your audience with half an idea.
They're unlikely to back it if they don't know what it is.

There are two types of crowdfunding -

1. **One-off projects**
   This is where you ask your fans to pre-order a product or back a project that you're working on. This could be an album or a DVD recording of your show. This has been used for freelancers, artists and entrepreneurs who wanted to let the free market system dictate if their work is worth creating. Please note, just because you don't raise the money you need the first time you do this kind of crowdfunding does **not** mean the work you were going to make is invalid or not valuable. It just means you haven't found enough people to back it.

2. **Ongoing projects**
   This is where you ask your fans to donate (or tip) you for creating ongoing streams of content. This is best used for someone who creates free online content who needs money to continue creating. YouTubers were the first to adopt this method of crowdfunding in order to turn off their adverts so they can focus on the work they're making. It is best viewed as a method to give your fans a way of paying you rather than "asking for money" because your biggest fans will want you to keep creating.

Each type of crowdfunding has its pros and cons and depending on what you're making or looking to create, but one option will clearly be more useful and respectful of your audience.

Remember, you're asking a person to pay for you to make something. No matter how much or little they decide to back you, you must show them all respect and be thankful.

By asking for money you're taking a fan's level of connection and commitment with you up a level. Think about it... you can be friends with someone for years and then ask them to lend you £10 or buy something off you. That level of trust and moment of negotiation helps build (and break) bonds. **So be careful with it.**

There is an old line about the civil courts being busy with former friends. Negotiate this difficult area and come out with your relationships staying friendly - **don't make enemies.** As with any transaction, make sure everyone knows what they are getting for their money. Under promise and over deliver if you can - but never the other way round.

Here are some pros and cons of crowdfunding in each method -

One off projects -

Pros	Cons
You can pre-sell the item before you've made it.	You have to do all of the work yourself.
You can build a better and stronger relationship with your Fans and Super Fans.	It is emotionally and physically demanding work (worrying nobody will back you etc).
You're in control: you can do and make anything in the way you want to.	Delivering the rewards for early backers takes a lot of time and effort and can take your energy away from creating the final project.
Getting funding from your audience is often quicker than asking for money from an investor or trying to get a "yes" from a production house.	It involves convincing a lot of people that you're worth buying from with no credible history of selling things.
Your Fans can directly influence what you're making and you can engage with them directly.	You might not make the funding and so have taken up to a month off paid work with little to no financial compensation.

Websites you should check out for one off crowdfunding -

- Kickstarter.com
- IndieGoGo.com
- PledgeMusic.com
- gogetfunding.com
- gofundme.com
- fundly.com

Ongoing Projects

Ongoing projects need funding in a totally different way. These methods are tailored to someone who wants to create content for a medium to longterm time period and needs a small budget for each thing they're making e.g. artists who create free online content but need to make money from it somehow such as people who make podcasts, YouTubers who make free videos, musicians who share their work on Spotify etc.

Pros	Cons
A budget upfront for any new / future work.	Adds pressure to an artist to create consistent content because it now becomes a job.
The knowledge that what you're doing is valued by a small selection of Super Fans.	The Fans can take away the funding at any time if they decide the value is not worth it for them or if they can't afford to continue funding you.
You're growing your own community of hardcore Fans.	Additional admin.
Getting paid for work that otherwise was getting done for free.	Delivering extra content / gifts to backers can take up a lot of time.

Websites you should check out for ongoing crowdfunding -

- Patreon.com
- PayPal.com

- seedandspark.com
- beaconreader.com
- gratipay.com

Crowdfunding in any form is best done by an artist with a core fan base or audience. There's little to no point in putting 1 video on YouTube and asking for funding for future ones. You've not proven you can do the work on a consistent basis and there's little to no connection between the creator and fan.

By engaging with your audience and being honest with them you can start to read the signs that you might have fans who are willing to fund the future of your work. If you have a handful of people who constantly rave about your work, share it and give you great feedback, then you might be in a position to think about crowdfunding.

Do not crowdfund unnecessarily. Asking for money when you don't need it or can't deliver something is the quickest way to losing fans and damaging your reputation. And your good reputation is the most valuable tool you have to starting a new relationship with a potential fan in your audience.

To sum up...

- Crowdfunding is the best way for artists to fund their work as it puts the power in the hands of their fans.
- Only you know the "best time" to crowdfund your next project or existing content production.
- Don't go to your audience with half an idea. They're unlikely to back it if they don't know what it is.
- There are two types of crowdfunding: One-off Projects and Ongoing Projects.
- Each type of crowdfunding has its pros and cons and depending on what you're making or looking to create, but one option will clearly be more useful and respectful of your audience.
- Remember, you're asking a person to pay for you to make something. No matter how much or little they decide to back you, you must show them all respect and be thankful.
- By asking for money you're taking a fan's level of connection and commitment with you up a level.
- Under promise and over deliver if you can - but never the other way round.
- Crowdfunding in any form is best done by an artist with a core fan base or audience.
- Do not crowdfund unnecessarily. Asking for money when you don't need it or can't deliver something is the quickest way to losing fans and damaging your reputation. And your good reputation is the most valuable tool you have to starting a new relationship with a potential fan in your audience.

One-off crowdfunding Examples.

Print Case Study: Shane Koyczan

Overview.
Shane Koyczan is a Canadian spoken word poet and writer. He is best known for writing about issues like bullying, cancer, death and eating disorders. His poems have helped many overcome depression, anxiety and suicidal thoughts.

Shane has built up an audience of over 124,000 Facebook Fans, 48,000 followers on Twitter, 255,000 subscribers on YouTube and an unknown number of email subscribers. Without allowing for crossover between platforms he has an audience of 427,000 people.

His free content comes in the form of YouTube videos of his poems, exclusive poems in his monthly newsletter and updates on Twitter and Facebook.

His latest poem was performed as a TED talk which has been viewed more than 2 million times in its first 2 years.

The 80:20 Principle.
In January 2015 Shane Koyczan launched a KickStrter crowdfunding campaign for his latest book of poems. His goal was $15,000 but by the end of the 30-day campaign he had raised $91,154 in pre-sales and donations.

Shane's total audience is approximately 427,000 people.

His KickStarter was funded by 1,688 people (**0.4% of his audience**). [2]

1,000 True Fans and Average Figures.

The book was funded by 1,688 of Shane's Fans. The average cost of a book of poetry is $12. To get the initial $15,000 he would have needed 1,250 fans to buy the book. To raise the $91,154 he got he would need to have sold 7,596 copies. By going direct to his loyal fan base online Shane made his campaign live in the online world (**Extremistan**) rather than limited to the physical world (**Mediocristan**) we can see that his audience were more than willing to give a larger amount of money on something they'd value.

The Curve.

If his campaign existed in the real world (**Mediocristan**) you would take the total donations ($77,888) and divide it by the number of people that donated (1,688) and get the average donation per person ($46.14).

If we look at the donations breakdown (below) we can see this is not the case —

Donation amount	Backers	Est. revenue
$1 or more	14	$14
$2 or more	1	$2
$3 or more	8	$24
$4 or more	1	$4
$5 or more	19	$95
$10 or more	96	$960
$18 or more	144	$2,592
$25 or more	219	$5,475
$30 or more	**413**	**$12,390**
$35 or more	267	$9,345
$50 or more	177	$8,850
$75 or more	**145**	**$10,875**
$75 or more	32	$2,400
$100 or more	17	$1,700
$100 or more	50	$5,000
$200 or more	35	$7,000
$250 or more	2	$500
$250 or more	0	$0
$250 or more	**1**	**$250**
$300 or more	**10**	**$3,000**
$500 or more	**5**	**$2,500**
$500 or more	**4**	**$2,000**
$1,000 or more	**7**	**$7,000**
$5,000	0	$0
$8,000	0	$0
$8,000	0	$0

  Because each donation amount is the set price or higher we do not know the specific amount individual people gave which is why the end value is an estimate (or the lowest revenue amount for that level).

If Shane sold the album at $12 he would have lost out on the $1099 donated by the people who gave less than $12 to help his campaign.

He might have sold 1,528 books to the people who donated more than $12, but this would have totaled $18,336… $72,818 less than he achieved by offering variable price points.

In blue is the highest revenue generating price point (**at least $30 or more given by 413 fans**). We can also see that his biggest Super Fans are willing to give several times both these amounts at the top end of the project (in orange).

He would have capped his Super Fans from giving the amount that reflects how much they value what he does (the red dashed line below. Fig 1 below shows that the number of Freeloading Fans doesn't change, the number of paying audience also stays the same but the amount they can give you is limited. This results in a loss of funding and revenue for the artists -

Fig 1.

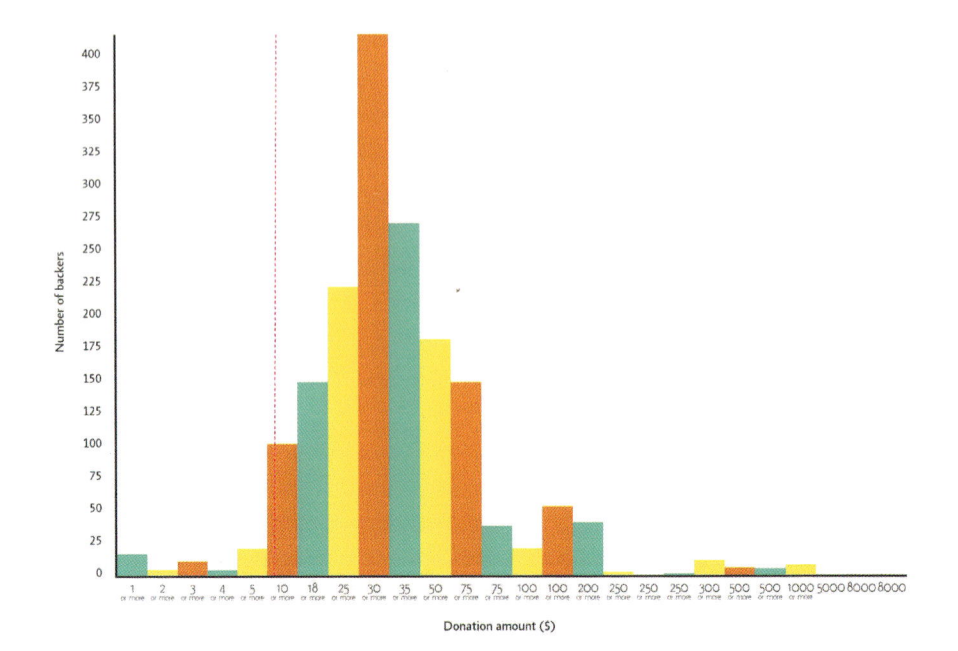

By allowing people to pay what they want Shane was able to fund his book with less people and give back to his Super Fans based on how much they value him.

The rewards ranged from "undying gratitude" to a copy of the book to copies of his out of print books to the option to have a book release party anywhere in America or Canada!

By using his personality as a brand and the online tools available to him Shane was able to offer amazing rewards and extra value simply by giving away extra stock of older products, signing his latest book and unpublished poems which didn't make it into the book. In the old world, these would be regarded as 'waste' products or an 'inventory problem'. In this new online world, they are vital tools for building and growing stronger relationships with Fans.

Ongoing crowdfunding examples

Music Case Study: Dodie Clark.

Overview
Dodie Clark is an English YouTube vlogger and musician. She created her account in February 2011 and posted her first video in April of the same year - an original song called "Rain". She now has nearly 300,000 subscribers on her channel and over 20 million views.

Although she sells t-shirts and CDs at gigs Dodie has managed to utilise her online fan base to help her to continue to create online content and share it for free.

The 80:20 Principle & 1,000 True Fans
Dodie has 289,000 subscribers on YouTube, 100,000 followers on Twitter and 21,000 Fans on Facebook.

Dodie's total audience is approximately 410,000 people (allowing for no crossover).

She currently has **710** Patrons donating **$954.90** per video.

She releases 1 video per week which means she makes **$3819.60** (**£2514.30**) per month on YouTube. This money comes from **0.17%** of her total audience. [3]

Patreon and why online adverts don't work.
Dodie has been on YouTube for 4 years and had more than 20 million views. If every single view was monetized (which it almost certainly wasn't) at £2 per 1,000 views (which is high) Dodie would have made £40,000 (around £10,000 per year).

With Patreon Dodie is earning approximately £30,171.60 per year and instead of her constantly chasing more views to earn more money she just needs to keep her Patrons happy which is a lot easier and more fun!

A mix of ongoing and one off crowdfunding examples -

Music Case Study: Julia Nunes.

Overview
Julia Nunes is a singer-songwriter who joined YouTube in March 2006. Since then she's uploaded dozens of videos showing her range of musical talents as well as music interests.

She's built up an audience of over 200,000 subscribers on YouTube, 35,000 Followers on Twitter and 67,000 Fans on Facebook. Without allowing for crossover between platforms she has an audience of nearly 300,000 people.

Her free content comes primarily in the form of her YouTube videos as well as her free-to-stream albums on Spotify. She also shares her tour updates with her fans on Twitter, Facebook and YouTube.

Longer Background
Julia joined YouTube and started uploading covers of songs she liked. After a few uploads the Bushman Ukulele Competition messaged her through the site to say she should enter. The prize was a free Ukulele if she won, which she did. This led to her first paid gig as a musician.

She uploaded an original song at the request of one of her early Fans. YouTube put her song on the front page. This led to a jump in views on her videos. This "shortcut" to temporary YouTube fame was the opposite of what she wanted:

> "I hated being seen by so many people who didn't like my stuff. YouTube comments are the most honest feedback you'll ever get. People don't hold back in there. I had a nose ring at the time. YouTube didn't like that."
> – JULIA NUNES.

Julia uploaded a cover of a Ben Folds song, he saw it and messaged her on MySpace to open for his band. Aside from this being a big opportunity, Ben Folds happened to be one of Julia's favourite musicians.

She recorded her first album in college with friends and the equipment from the school. She thought it was bad but she felt so connected with her Fans she released it anyway and they loved it.

In 2008 YouTube held an event called "YouTube Live" which Julia took part in. She thought this would be her "big break" but found it didn't help her at all.

Later that year her sister organised a UK tour for her (before she'd toured anywhere in America). This helped her gain more Fans and connect with the existing ones who didn't live anywhere near her hometown in America.

An intern at the company organising Bonnaroo (a music festival in the US) was asked to find small, unknown bands to play "short filler spots" during the festival. Despite having an ever-increasing fanbase on YouTube this intern put her name forward as an "unknown" after watching her YouTube videos. She played several shows during the weekend for music lovers that helped her gain good exposure and Fans of her work.

She recorded an EP with a band called Pompamous and then went out every weekend and played shows with her songs and covers. She toured the East / West coast and the UK (2nd time). Opened for the alternative dance duo Matt and Kim at the River Fusion Festival as well as Kevin Bacon.

She went back to Bonnaroo the following year to play a feature length set. Before arriving she Tweeted the band Weezer saying "hey, come play this song with me during my set" and a link to a cover she did of their song "Trippin Down The Freeway". They replied saying "No. You come play this song with us during our set." Which she did.

Julia made a video where she got her Fans to lip sync to a song. One of these Fans submitted a video that had a Ben Kweller poster in the background. Just before Ben went on tour one of Julia's fans sent Ben the video and said "Your fans like Julia as well…" and he took Julia as his opening act on 24 shows.

FOX TV asked Julia to play herself in a TV show. She was the singer at a wedding. She needed a good recording of the song so asked her friends from college. Her friend Zack helped her record the song quickly for the show. Zack told Julia he liked working with her, we should do it again sometime, Julia said "I'm looking into recording an 18-song album…" Later that year Zack and Julia produced her next album which she funded through KickStarter.

> "I offered things that I would want from my favourite musicians which is why I think my KickStarter was so successful."
> – JULIA.

Her fans loved her music so much and gave her $80,000 in 30 days through KickStarter. This story caught the eye of Conan O'Brien who offered her to be the musical guest just before the album release date. Which she did.

The 80:20 Principle
In June 2011 Julia Nunes launched a KickStarter page to fund her 4th album. Her goal was $15,000 but within the first 24 hours of it going live she already had $19,000. At the end of the 30-day project she had $77,888 in donations, at the time this was the third most-funded music project in Kickstarter's history.

Julia's total audience is approximately 300,000 people.

Her KickStarter was funded by 1,685 people (**0.56% of her audience**). [4]

1,000 True Fans and Average Figures.
The album was funded through 1,685 of Julia's Fans. An average album in a shop costs $15, to achieve $77,888 she would need 5,192 people (except, of course, putting an album in a shop has production overheads to factor in so it would actually be a lot more than this). But because she went direct to her loyal audience and made her project available online (Extremistan) rather than limited to the physical world (Mediocristan) we can see that her audience were more than willing to give a larger amount of money on something they'd value.

The Curve
If her project existed in the real world (Mediocristan) you would take the total donations ($77,888) and divide it by the number of people that donated (1,685) and get the average donation per person ($46.22).

If we look at the donations breakdown (below) we can see this is not the case —

Donation amount	Backers	Est. revenue
$1 or more	39	$39
$10 or more	484	$4,840
$30 or more	454	$13,620
$50 or more	**378**	**$18,900**
$75 or more	**218 (limited to 250)**	**$16,350**
$100 or more	65	$6,500
$150 or more	4	$600
$250 or more	1	$250
$250 or more	4 (limited to 5)	$1,000
$300 or more	1 (limited to 5)	$300
$675 or more	**7**	**$4,725**
$1,000 or more	**3 (limited to 5)**	**$3,000**
$2,500 or more	**2**	**$5,000**

Because each donation amount is the set price or higher we do not know the specific amount individual people gave which is why the end value is an estimate (or the lowest revenue amount for that level).

If Julia sold the album at $15 she would have lost out on the $39 donated by the people who gave $1 to help her along and $4,840 donated by those giving her $10.

She might have made 1,162 sales of the CD from the rest of the backers totalling $17,430… $60,458 less than she achieved by offering variable price points.

In **blue** is the highest revenue generating price point ($50) but we can see she got nearly the same amount from over **150 less people at the $75 price point** (in **red**). We can also see that her biggest Super Fans are willing to give several times both these amounts at the top end of the project (in **orange**).

She would have capped her Super Fans from giving the amount that reflects how much they value what she does (the **red dashed line** below). Fig 1 below shows that the number of Freeloading fans doesn't change, the number of paying audience also stays the same but the amount they can give you is limited. This results in a loss of funding and revenue for the artists -

Fig 1.

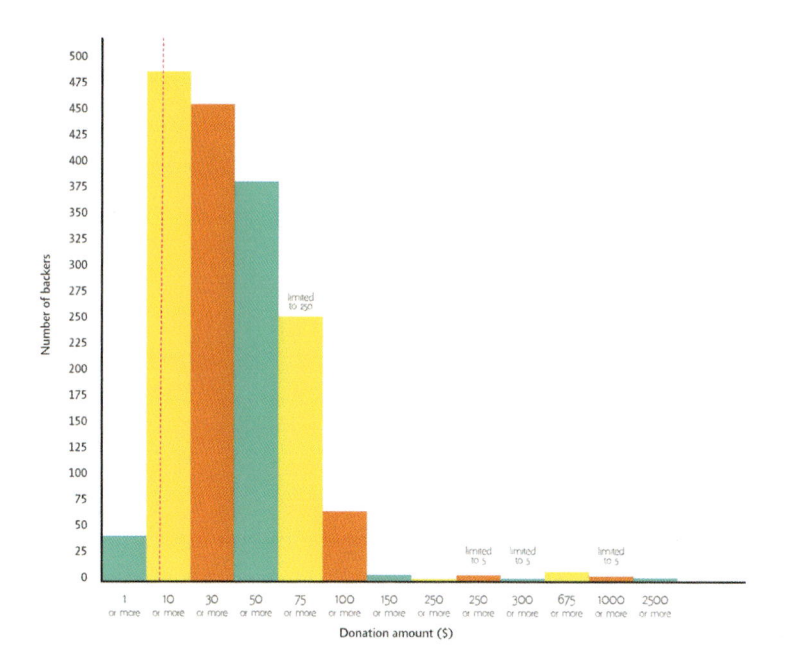

By allowing people to pay what they want Julia was able to fund her album with fewer people and give back to her Super Fans based on how much they value her.

Rewards ranged from gratitude to the digital version of the CD right up to handwritten lyrics and a Skype concert or music lesson.

By using the online tools at her disposal and intelligent marketing she added value to the existing product by giving away copies of her first albums and reprinting out of issue t-shirts. This means she pre-sold the merchandise, lowering her risk, and didn't have to create anything new as the designs already had been made.

She signed all the physical albums for the early backers. This is an inexpensive but personal way of giving back to people who first backed her campaign.

Patreon and why online adverts don't work.
After 7 years on YouTube Julia launched her Patreon page in which she explained why she needs the money for her videos - a budget and the knowledge that she can pay her rent, which previously she would have to do live shows to make the money to do. Additionally she offered 4 price points so her Patrons can give at the level they value her work.

She launched the page in May 2013 and within a year 315 Fans (that's around 1 new Patron per day) were giving her $1,732.11 per video. She uploads an average of 2 videos per month meaning her yearly YouTube video creation budget is **£41,570.64**. That's before her live shows or merchandise sales.

In April 2014 Julia's total video views was **54,385,534**. At £2 CPM (per 1,000 views, which is very high) her videos advert revenue would have made her an estimated **£13,596.38** over 8 years - £1699.54 per year.

> "Never before have we been able to offer our best thing, which is making videos, the way other artists offer their best thing. We've had to stick with their model of concerts and albums to make a living. I know I've forgone making a video in favour of making a tour or going into the studio because that's how you make money. You sell MP3s. But making music has never guaranteed that someone will buy it. Piracy is not going away and I think that's good. If you can't afford music, I still want you to hear my music."
> – JULIA NUNES. [5]

Adverts devalue content
As of June 2014 Julia had 54,690,021 views on her videos.

At $2 CPM* (cost per thousand views) she should have earned $54,690.02 over the past 8 years (if every single view was monetized, which they're not).

In 2011 it took Julia 30 days to get her top 1,685 fans to give her $77,888. This is £23,197.98 more than 8 years of videos would have earned her.

Clearly advertising doesn't work for Julia even with her large viewing numbers.

*$2 is a very high CPM

Reasons why people will pay for free content

> "I had built up such a great connection with my fans that they wanted me to make and sell them an album."
> – JULIA NUNES.

CHAPTER 14
First Steps / Devising Own Targets.

By now you should be able to see more clearly the path towards becoming a sustainable artist.

To get you started you should look back at your own mission statement which you filled out at the start of the book... is it still the same thing for you? If it is, great! If it has changed, now is the time to write a new mission statement below.

I am a _____

From my audience I want

_____

_____

_____

_____

_____

Based on what you've written above you should be able to pick a platform to showcase your work. Your content should dictate where you upload your work and not which platform has the highest number of people. For example, Facebook is the biggest social network in terms of users, but to upload your album there as a musician would not make sense even if there's more people on that website vs Spotify. Here's a little guide which should help you get started.

I am a...	I produce...	Platform(s) which might work for me...
Musician	Music	Spotify, YouTube, Last.FM
Comedian	Video sketches	YouTube, Vine
Director	Short films	YouTube, Vine
Photographer	Photos	Instagram, Flickr, Pinterest
Chef	Video / written recipes	YouTube, Facebook, Instagram
Make up artist	Video tutorials	YouTube, Instagram, Vine

A few things to remember...

When you join any social media platform there's probably a pre-existing community on the platform. So it's a good idea to invest time in searching for people who do something similar to you and supporting them - there's enough room for everyone.

When I decided to change the direction of my Twitter account to host throwaway jokes I started by searching for people who were funny on the site and following them. I'd ReTweet anything I thought was great and replied when they asked questions. Slowly I built up some solid friendships on the site and we have all since helped each other in our own projects.

You are trying to connect with your audience but you are also trying to connect with your peers. Above all you're trying to connect with people. Remember that when you're staring blankly at the number of Followers or Fans you have.

I keep putting stuff online and I'm getting nowhere...

Rome wasn't built in a day and neither will your fan base be. You need to keep creating, sharing and networking with your peers. If you are struggling to find an audience for what you do you can always join link sharing sites and share your work in there. Do not just copy/paste links to your work and think that's enough.

Sites like Reddit, Digg and StumbleUpon are social bookmarking sites which allow you (as a creator) to share your work in pre-existing niche communities who in turn might want to become Fans of what you do. The key to these sites is taking part in the discussions, establishing yourself as a thought leader or someone who knows and shares great content so people trust that what you share is worth their time. This reputation takes time and effort, but is worth it in the long run.

I've tried social bookmarking… where else can I look for my audience?

Your content should be niche and specific and therefore be appealing to subgroups of the internet. You need to find those people and convince them you're worth listening to. As we've seen in **Chapter 7: How can you be unique in your field?** the TV industrial complex doesn't work… so we need to aim at the fringes and not at the mass market.

1. **Identify 3-5 subcultures you belong to.**
   Think long and hard about this. If you're a comedian for example this doesn't have to be related to the jokes. I think this is where most people fall down. The subculture could be golf (for example) but you might have no golfing jokes… however the people who also like golf have something in common with you beyond golf which attracts them to that sport. It could be a way of life, big green fields or something else (I'm not an expert at golf). So first step, find your subcultures.
2. **Contact the right person in that group.**
   You might have a friend in it already or have a friend of a friend in it who can help. The "degrees of separation" have become easier since social media has allowed us all to talk and stay in touch with people. So post on your Facebook wall / Twitter feeds asking if anyone is already in a community you want to be a part of or talk to (this is NOT you taking without giving, you shouldn't expect to just share your

content to people. This is you joining a community or asking for a favour of one you're already in).

3. **Research the places they go for information**
Podcasts, blogs, news sites, event listings etc. Where do the golfers (I'm sticking with golf for some reason) go to find out about events or interesting industry news? It could be a newsletter or a twitter feed. You can even ask your friend in the community "where do you get your information about X?".

4. **Engage with the community**
Subscribe to the podcast and comment on the blog posts. Be seen to be sharing the links and reply to others who are asking questions in relation to the posts. You're a person and so are they.

5. **Ask for help.**
When you feel comfortable say to this group of people or person "I've got a video tutorial / blog post / podcast etc I'd love to just tell you about it". Think of it like digital flyering. Only difference is you've already got a relationship with that person / group which means they're likely to give you a minute more than a stranger on the street. You've caught them at the right time when they have a minute to read / listen and process your message. On the street... they might be in a hurry to get somewhere. You've less time and less chance they'll care. Just ask the person who runs the blog / podcast etc. if they can mention your show / preview / project. They might say no, they might say yes. You never know until you ask.

6. **Thank them and remain in contact**
At the end of my Brighton Fringe 2015 run I gave the bar staff a box of Celebrations. They said nobody else had done that and it was sweet. This made me happy and sad... given the number of shows happening in the venue I thought I wouldn't be alone in trying to remain friends with people who ultimately have helped my show. I also emailed every company who let me put a poster up individually thanking them for their help and saying I'd pop in when I am back down. I'm also going to add them to my blog post about the Brighton Fringe as a thank you and form of free advertising for them. To remain in contact you can start a newsletter, or a Twitter feed or a Facebook group... pick the one that works for you. Learn from your community research. Did

you find that most people get information from Facebook Groups or Twitter? Then join that platform. Don't just make an account for the hell of it.

Online I add all my previous podcast guests on a social media site and email them on a regular basis (maybe once every couple of months unless there's something important I think they'll be interested in). This is for two reasons, firstly I am actually interested in how they are and secondly it keeps me in their minds.

Thank you

Finally, thank you for reading my book. It means a lot to me that you've got this far - I buy far too many books and don't get around to reading all of them. It's great to see your dedication to your work and I really hope you got some value out of it.

If you'd like to send me a message, feel free to do so via email - simon.m.caine@gmail.com or on twitter @ThisMadeMeCool. I'm always happy to hear constructive feedback.

This copy of the book I self published. It has taken me just over two years to write, research and get into your hands. As an "unknown author" (as the publishing industry likes to call me) I have to do everything myself from getting the book written to marketing to the blurb on the back cover. Everything.

The fact you took a chance on me and this project means the world and I can't thank you enough.

The book is available on Amazon. It would be great if you could give it a honest review. As you now know, online reviews are basically word-of-mouth that never goes away and they can make or break a book online. So if you enjoyed it, please review it. If you didn't… feel free to email me your hate.

Chapter 1: How to make money out of your creativity?
[1] https://www.youtube.com/user/doddleoddle
[2] https://www.youtube.com/user/LazyPillow

Chapter 3: Where are you at the moment?
[1] http://amzn.to/1qGVzLU
[2] https://bundles.bittorrent.com/bundles/a1e9a2153051b92d00b27903f-cbdc2c530b5c4a044935c1ed7bbdf60e7b307db
[3] https://en.wikipedia.org/wiki/Sixto_Rodriguez
[4] http://amzn.to/1SzHARA
[5] http://kck.st/1NG5Zk4
[6] http://kck.st/1bvzm8M
[7] http://kck.st/1MNTCaQ
[8] http://kck.st/17SMAO4
[9] http://www.virginmoneygiving.com/team/ComedyCollectiveChristmas
[10] https://www.patreon.com/jackconte
[11] https://www.patreon.com/comedybutton

Chapter 5: Why you shouldn't aim for the mainstream.
[1] http://amzn.to/1NG6ElF
[2] http://fortune.com/2012/07/30/amazons-recommendation-secret/

Chapter 6: How many fans do you really need?
[1] http://kk.org/thetechnium/1000-true-fans/
[2] http://kck.st/1Vr4VIO
[3] http://bit.ly/1VHVh52
[4] http://amzn.to/1qGWJH7

Chapter 7: How can you be unique in your field?
[1] http://amzn.to/26kOt0k
[2] http://amzn.to/1T4b4V3
[3] http://www.legislation.gov.uk/uksi/2003/2426/contents/made
[4] https://www.patreon.com/SmoothMcGroove?ty=h
[5] http://amzn.to/1TnSI4b
[6] *http://www.theguardian.com/media/2010/jul/20/times-paywall-readership*

[7] http://bit.ly/1YLJArx
[8] https://www.patreon.com/hannahwitton
[9] http://blog.bittorrent.com/2013/04/04/your-book-is-a-startup-tim-ferriss-the-4-hour-chef-and-the-bittorrent-publishing-model/

Chapter 8: Why advertising undervalues content.
[1] http://reut.rs/215zHa2

Chapter 11: Why paywalls are the worst thing online.
[1] https://www.patreon.com/AskTheIndustryPodcast

Chapter 12: Vanity Figures.
[1] http://amzn.to/22UuJfF

Chapter 13: A Quick Guide to Crowdfunding.
[1] http://amzn.to/1VHWJV5
[2] https://www.kickstarter.com/projects/326083440/a-bruise-on-light
[3] https://www.patreon.com/doddleoddle?ty=h
[4] http://kck.st/1XNsKbu
[5] https://www.patreon.com/julianunes?ty=h

How To Make A Living By Working For Free